PRISONS
IN CANADA

PRISONS IN CANADA

by Luc Gosselin

173654122

BLACK ROSE BOOKS   Montréal

Copyright 1982 ©
BLACK ROSE BOOKS LTD.

Originally published in 1977 as
Les pénitenciers: un système à abattre.

Les Éditions Coopératives
    Albert St-Martin.

Black Rose Books No J-63
Hardcover — ISBN: 0-919619-12-1
Paperback — ISBN: 0-919619-11-8

Canadian Cataloguing in Publication Data

Gosselin, Luc, 1946 —
    Prisons in Canada

Translation of: Les pénitenciers.
ISBN 0-919619-12-1 (bound).   ISBN 0-919619-11-8 (pbk.)

1. Prisons — Canada.
I. Title.

HV9507.G6813   365'.971   C82-090129-6

Cover design: Cliff Harper
BLACK ROSE BOOKS LTD.
3981 boulevard St-Laurent,
Montréal, H2W 1Y5, Québec
Printed and bound in Québec, Canada

Dedication

In memory of Jean-Paul Mercier, whom the prisons
could not subdue, murdered by 20 policemen
on October 31, 1976.

Dedication

Table of Contents

Photo Credit: Pierre Gaudard. St.Vincent de Paul, Laval Institution, Super Maximum.

By Way of a Preface

In the 18th century, John Howard sought to reform the prison system; today Luc Gosselin seeks to abolish it. In this eloquent, sometimes impassioned plea, marked throughout by his fundamental respect for all human beings, he presents, page after page, the facts to back his argument for the destruction of those horrifying institutions where we permit the state, through our collective indifference, to lock people up and cause them to suffer in a system that offers little hope of rehabilitation.

Luc Gosselin has written a critical analysis of the penal system of this country, not a history of the sentences and punishments inflicted on "delinquent" citizens. His detailed examination shows us how this entirely repressive system came to be established, and why — for the protection and reinforcement of a social order whose primary beneficiaries are lawyers, judges and politicians. For there can be no doubt: the penal system is one of the instruments openly used by the state (along with the police, the judicial system and, when necessary, the army) to maintain its authority. This is particularly obvious in times of crisis (the insurrection of 1837-38, the 1917 conscription crisis, the Winnipeg General Strike of 1919, the great economic crisis of 1929-37, the events of 1970), times when the legitimacy and the stability of the authorities are being challenged by rising social forces.

Luc Gosselin's work fills an important gap: nobody to date has posed the problem in such clear terms. This book, therefore, may cause you to discover a whole new world, an almost unimaginable world.... The walls encircling our penitentiaries are there to reassure you (the "bad" people are shut up inside so that we, the "good" people, may live outside in freedom), to cause you to forget about those who have been swallowed up, to hide from you the regime to which they are being subjected. We can testify to it; we have lived it.

But it must not be forgotten that this book deals with only one aspect of the major social problem constituted by our system of detention. It limits itself to the penitentiaries, that is, to the federal institutions which house those whom the judicial apparatus has sentenced to two or more years of incarceration. But there are all the other prisoners as well, the people who are sentenced to a few days or a few months and who end up in the often ancient and unsanitary common prisons. Don't think that prisons are for "other" people: more than one million adult Canadians have done time. And that figure excludes the past and present population of the repressive institutions for adolescents: the "correction" centres, the "re-education" centres, the "welcome" centres.

If there are so many offenders — for example, citizens who question the values upheld by the established social order — it is not because of sheer wickedness on their part, but because that social order does not deserve respect and forces a great many people to survive by their wits. These prisons reflect the society which constructs them.

We must therefore make a collective effort to come up with alternatives to the system of punitive imprisonment (whose failure is self-evident, given the rate of recidivism). Alternatives do exist, even though the state, mainly because of the considerable pressure exerted by those who benefit from the present system, is reluctant to acknowledge them.

Dejudicialization is the first possibility. Why involve the courts and mobilize the whole repressive apparatus to deal with minor offences whose damages are reparable? Why put the "offenders" through a series of procedures which inevitably embitter them and convince them that they have a score to settle with society upon their liberation (and they *will* eventually be liberated, whatever their sentence)?

And why, if society's motive is the prevention of more crime rather than revenge, imprison a person any longer than the brief period of time needed to make them understand that they have behaved badly (if that is indeed the case)? Montesquieu's brilliant contribution to penal theory was the observation that the degree of fear engendered by a given punishment lay in the comparison between that punishment and other known penalties. Thus, if the general level of punishment were to be reduced, no truly severe punishment would be necessary thereafter. The minimum punishment inflicted ought to be just enough to have a strong effect upon the offender.

In the 18th century, Montesquieu said: "Any punishment whose need is not absolute is an act of tyranny." One century later, Beccaria echoed the same theme: "Any act of authority exercised by one man over another is tyrannical unless it is absolutely necessary."

Why imprison people at all? Why follow a path that is so negative, so purely repressive, when it is possible to offer positive compensation instead? Take the case of vandalism: the persons involved could be set to do community work which would lead them to question themselves in a positive fashion about their contribution to the community. Being put into any one of a number of popular organizations—food co-op, community day-care centre, etc.—would encourage such persons to begin to question the egotistical motivations (the look-out-for-number-one attitude that characterizes capitalist society) behind their present behaviour patterns, and to replace them with the much more progressive values of solidarity, fraternity, and respect for others.

Measures like these would allow us to empty our prisons of the majority of their present occupants. Collectively, we would save tens of millions of ill-used tax dollars. Furthermore, we would create enough room to offer individualized treatment—though not necessarily in prisons—to those whose criminal behaviour truly requires corrective social action.

We have no illusions about the potential of partial

reform and so, in company with those now suffering the loss of their liberties, we demand the abolition of the penitentiaries. Nonetheless, perhaps because we have lived in those places and because we are human beings, we still hope that changes will be made to the system as quickly as possible.

History is a daily affair. It is the sum of our daily lives. It is therefore up to us to write our own history, to *make* it, by involving ourselves resolutely in the battle for progress and the triumph of respect for human beings. And so, the Bureau for Prisoners' Rights will receive authors' royalties from the sale of this book. May our comrades soon leave places like Archambault, Leclerc, and Cowanswille to join us in the outside world, and a normal existence.

Dr. Raymond Boyer
Claude Larivière

16

Foreword

In Canada, as in the rest of the world, the repressive apparatus of the state and its keystone, the penal institution, is the voice of authority that regulates social control. The teeming numbers locked away in jail are the counterpoint to the regime's slogans, whether that slogan promises a "just society" or "revolutionary power."

The truth of this claim is easily demonstrated.

The State segregates men and women, locks them up in cages, tortures them, traps them in a cycle of misery, repeated offences and suicide — all on the pretext of a criminal act, and in the name of the common good.

Since only a minority of the population ever experiences the horror of prison life, the annihilating nature of the procedure is of course both disguised and denied. Barriers are thrown up to limit information and bowdlerize revelations. Entries and exits are controlled, mail censored, visitors screened. First-hand witnesses are hived off. Thus, prison personnel, for a whole variety of reasons, form a homogeneous, monolithic, in-turned bloc. The prisoners, or ex-prisoners — condemned, marginalized, reduced to silence — have a choice between radical action and oblivion. In other words, between spectacular death or slow death... And should their testimony somehow burst upon the world one day, the public has had long conditioning in how to react: the cruelty of the punishment never has the impact of the alleged crime.

Hardly surprising, therefore, that most people make do with a superficial study of prison realities — a study whose content, obviously, has been determined by the authorities.

But when we go beyond that superficial look — when we study the social, political and economic context of this repressive institution, when we analyze the life of the salaried worker (that refined form of slavery), workers' conditions, socio-economic disparities, the degradation of the environment, the incredible accumulation of wealth and power in the hands of the few (when the world's hungry press us on all sides), the frenzied arms race, the polarization born of armed exploitation — then some common threads begin to emerge.

Prisons are not maintained for the common good, but for bourgeois power. This term, "bourgeois power," includes the monopolist bourgeoisie of western countries which owns the means of production, the state bourgeoisie of so-called "socialist" countries which controls the means of production, and the "comprador" bourgeoisie of Third World countries which plays valet to the interests of the other two bourgeoisies. And all this, so that international capital may continue to accumulate, so that the labour of the working class may be appropriated. So that exploitation may continue.

But we can take a long time to reach this understanding of social structures.

The dominant ideology — that is, the vision of the world imposed by the leading class of the bourgeoisie — has developed mechanisms and patterns of thought which justify and legitimize these actions.

When it comes to prisons and penitentiaries, the authorities easily find both source and force for their stand in the criminology argument: "crimes" are committed; "criminals" commit them. It is obviously necessary that the guilty parties be detained somewhere. The penitentiary, therefore, is designated as the place for punishment, dialogue and "rehabilitation." It may be imperfect (every report issued in the last 150 years makes this abundantly clear), but it is necessary.

Whenever problems arise within the institution, they

are translated into administrative terms: budgets, population, organization. The fundamentals of the system are unquestioned.

Debate about the institution is not only allowed, it is encouraged. But the State makes sure that this debate is limited to the classic confrontation between progressive and coercive approaches. Psychologists and chaplains on one side; wardens, police and right-wing politicians on the other.

Thus the endless monologues by inmates, administrative authorities and specialists always end up focusing on what is normality, danger, rehabilitation, the rising rate of criminality, and the protection of the public interest. The political reasons for the system of imprisonment itself never come into the open.

This book takes a radical approach to the penitentiary phenomenon. It contrasts the justifications for the system with the observed effects of that system, and reveals the politico-economic reasons for incarceration. We wish the daily battles of the inmates to be understood in a larger perspective, and their struggle to take its place among the other battles of the working class.

Introduction

"Before long they will have more prisons in Canada than MacDonald's has hamburger outlets."

D.W. McLean[1]

On October 21, 1976, the solicitor-general of Canada, Mr. Francis Fox, presented a motion in the House of Commons calling for the creation of a sub-committee of inquiry into the nation's penitentiaries. The motion, which received unanimous approval, was justified on three main grounds.

First, three riots had taken place the previous month in three different maximum-security institutions — New Westminster in British Columbia, Laval in Québec and Millhaven in Ontario. These riots were only the symptoms of a deeper malaise percolating through the system, especially in the maximum-security institutions.

Second, the creation of just such a committee of inquiry had been one of the conditions for the liberation of hostages taken at New Westminster. The prisoners' demand had been seconded by the citizens' committee there.

Finally and most importantly, the commission of inquiry, through the classic process of consultation, was intended to create as favourable a public climate as possible for the ultra-repressive measures which Fox planned soon to

20

introduce to the system: Bill C-51 (authorizing indeterminate sentences), the construction of 24 new penitentiaries, and the application of the recommendations contained in the report of "the Task Force on the Creation of an Integrated Canadian Corrections Service," created in 1973[2].

The inquiry, chaired by Mr. Mark MacGuigan*, spent some six months waltzing from one end of the country to the other, asking inmates, wardens, citizens and senior administrators their opinions on prisons in general and penitentiaries in particular.

The mandate was as follows:

> "*Ordered*, — That the Sub-committee on the Penitentiary System in Canada have the power to inquire into the system of maximum security institutions maintained by the Canadian Penitentiary Service and such other institutions as the Committee deems advisable, including:
>
> (a) the adequacy of security procedures and arrangements, custodial facilities and correctional programmes pertaining to such institutions,
>
> (b) the special problems faced by staff and management in the administration of such institutions,
>
> (c) the need for, the role and composition of Citizens Advisory Committees attached to such institutions,
>
> (d) the need for, the role and composition of Inmates Committees in such institutions,
>
> and any other matter that the Sub-committee may consider relevant to the proper administration of such institutions, having regard to the recent disturbances that have taken place in the British Columbia, Laval and Millhaven Penitentiaries; and to invite the views of interested parties and the public on these matters..."[3]

---

* At present, Mr. MacGuigan is Minister of External Relations for Canada. *Publisher's note*, June 1982.

Most of the hearings were compiled in forty-four volumes of minutes.* We shall be drawing upon these minutes in the course of this present study.

The ultimate recommendations of the sub-committee were easy enough the predict — so easy that one could have taken instead the conclusions and recommendations of the 1927 annual report of the Superintendent of Penitentiaries. The differences are negligible.

For at the end of his 1927 report to the minister of justice of the day, M.W.S. Hughes wrote that certain steps were urgently required:

> "1. Institutions for the selection and sorting classification of detained persons are strongly recommended.
>
> 2. The reopening of the hospital for criminals afflicted with mental alienation.
>
> 3. The separation of hardened criminals.
>
> 4. That the government furnish more work for inmates.
>
> 5. Payment of a salary for work done by inmates whose conduct is good.
>
> 6. Find work for inmates before their liberation.
>
> 7. Training of personnel before they are put in charge of the inmates.
>
> 8. That the directors of a penitentiary be authorized to maintain good discipline in the same way as in the Royal Mounted Police."[4]

Fifty years have not wrought many changes in the pious statements mouthed by those responsible for the repression.

The first part of this book, *The Great Contradiction*, documents the gap between the authorities' justification for penitentiaries (as found in official reports, inquiries, etc.) and their observed effects (increased violence, and a milieu that itself breeds new crime). The basic hypothesis is that the true but undeclared objectives of the penitentiary system can be

---

* *Minutes of the Proceedings and Evidence of the Sub-Committee on the Penitentiary System in Canada*, Ottawa, 1977 — translator's note.

seen in its effects. After all, it is highly unlikely that an institution could survive and grow for more than 150 years if it were in fact fulfilling only a tiny fraction of its mandate.

The second part of this book is entitled *The Historical Link*. It sketches the birth and evolution of the penitentiary system throughout the world and in Canada, tracing the waves of rethinking, reform and modification to date. The penitentiary, in other words, is not an isolated, static event in history, untouched (as the authorities like to claim) by political considerations. This historical perspective reinforces our basic working premise, and allows us, in the third part of the book, to analyze the political role of prisons.

PART ONE:
The Great Contradiction

Photo Credit: Pierre Gaudard. Reception Centre (Maximum).

CHAPTER 1
The Paper Chain of Reports

During his testimony to the MacGuigan sub-committee, M.J.M. Murphy, regional director for British Columbia, stated that there had been a deluge of reports through the years, starting with the Brown report published only 14 years after the opening of the first Canadian penitentiary in Kingston in 1835, then an inquiry into *that* inquiry and "then we went to 1876, 1920, 1936, 1937, 1953, 1965, 1970, 1973 and 1977, so, it is not our first round of inquiries... We have also had a number of annual reports. Probably we can list forty..."[5]

Some of these reports set the tone for an entire era — the Archambault report of 1938, for example. It presented an interesting definition of the "acceptable" penitentiary of the future, and its programme.

According to Archambault, the system was to rest on three principles:

"I. Means should be devised, and adequate policies adopted, which would tend to prevent crimes from being committed;

II. A system should be evolved, and put into force, which would prevent the repetition of crime, bring about the reformation and rehabilitation of those who have committed crimes, and take care of those who have been released from prisons;

III. Measures should be enacted that would debar habitual criminals from the opportunity to continue the commission of crimes."[6]

Guided by these three principles, the Archambault commission undertook, from October 1936 to December 1937, the most extensive study ever made of the Canadian Penitentiary Service.

They visited the seven federal institutions of the day and, in their many private hearings, sought out the opinions of judges, magistrates, former employees, police officers and former inmates. Public hearings were held in the major Canadian cities, and they visited foreign institutions as well in a tour through England, Scotland, Holland, Belgium, Germany, Switzerland, France and, of course, the United States.

A grand total of 1840 inmates and 200 officers testified under oath. As well, the inquirers sifted through 1200 letters, diaries, manuscripts, reports and other documents.

Eighty-eight separate recommendations emerged from this prodigious work. Most of them dealt with administrative matters: control, administrative reorganization, classification, prison discipline, use of firearms, recreation, education, medical services, religious services, penal work, prisoner remuneration. A few of them touched on the judicial process itself: amendments to the Criminal Code, the suppression of crime, parole. Some of the recommended changes, measures designed to nudge the institutions out of the Middle Ages and into the twentieth century, were only put into practice 30 years later by the MacLeod administration—for example, the classification of institutions by degree of security, and the abolition of corporal punishment.

The inquiry served to defuse the widespread condition of near rebellion in prisons at the time, and to introduce a concept of reform which was not, however, to take effect for several more decades.

And it did something else, something on the hidden agenda of all inquiries: it soothed public opinion. Riots, escapes and hostage-takings can all disturb social stability by frightening the "good" citizens. It is therefore highly profitable, politically speaking, for the authorities to order an inquiry whenever such events occur with heightened frequency. (But the order for the inquiry, of course, must be couched in terms that show the situation is well under control...)

In 1969, after numerous reports and numerous acts of violence inside prison walls, the Canadian government once again ordered an "in-depth study."

This time, it was Judge Ouimet who took on the responsibility. His committee tackled a good many problems, and considered itself to be a progressive group.

The discussion about the prison process, however, was conducted within the traditional framework.

> "A primary aim of the prison is to re-educate people to live law-abiding lives in the community... The traditional prison tears the individual away from such family, community, education and employment responsibilities and isolates him in an abnormal society where he is exposed to a criminal value system... It is difficult to conceive a device less suited to preparing people to live in the normal community than the traditional prison."[7]

Ouimet, like all his predecessors, issued a warning as old as the institution he was called upon to examine:

> "A concerted effort should be made to treat these people while they are in custody, but it must be recognized that the primary aim is protection of society through their segregation."[8]

And then he uttered the customary recommendations:

> "A successful prison system requires efficient classification so that the inmate will be dealt with in the most productive way feasible."[9]

And he continued:

> "Treatment and training are closely related and together they constitute a series of progressive re-educative experiences for the inmate which promote his identification with non-criminal so-

29

ciety and with goals sanctioned by the community."[10]

The report has certain interesting comments on the subject of treatment, as we shall see later. It calls for:

"The creation of a general atmosphere, felt by inmates and staff alike, that fosters both a belief that the inmates' attitudes and social habits can be changed and a determination to bring this about."[11]

As one of the appendices makes clear, the judge's interest in the new techniques of the social sciences did not preclude continuing reliance on more traditional techniques, such as hope in the Great Beyond:

"The Canadian Correctional Chaplains Association is integrally involved in the process of corrections and contributes the theological perspective... The approach of theology to corrections is not only a matter of penitence but moves towards renewal and redemption."[12]

(And for those who think this attitude belongs to the past, albeit the recent past, let it be noted that ever since 1974, this devoted group of people has enjoyed a separate division of their own, the chaplaincy service, within the programmes of the Canadian Penitentiary Service!)

Like all its predecessors, the Ouimet report failed to question the basics of the penitentiary system. It was yet another affirmation of the wisdom of that system and its institutions.

Foucault, in his admirable work, *Surveiller et punir*,* makes an excellent seven-point summary of what, for every régime, has constituted "desirable" penitentiary conditions:

"1. Penal detention has as one of its essential functions the transformation of the behaviour of the individual.

2. The inmates ought to be isolated, or at least segregated by the gravity of their offence, but especially by age, temperament, correctional techniques to be used upon them, and the stage

_____

* *Surveillance and Punishment*—translator's note.

30

of their transformation.

3. Sentences should vary according to the temperament of the inmate concerned, the results being obtained, progress and setbacks.

4. Work should be one of the essential elements of the transformation and socialization of the inmate.

5. Education of the inmate by the State is both an indispensable precaution to be taken for society's sake and an obligation to the inmate.

6. The prison system ought to be at least partially controlled and administered by specialized personnel having the moral capabilities and the techniques to watch over the proper training of the inmates.

7. Imprisonment must be followed by measures of control and assistance until the definitive re-adaptation of the former inmate."[13]

It is therefore unnecessary to examine all the literature—such as the Fauteux report (1956), the report of "the joint special committee of the Senate and the House of Commons on Penitentiaries" (1966), the Swackhamer report (1972), the Mohr report (1971), the "report by the corrections inquirer" (1975) and the Vantour report (1975)—because each of them, whatever its own particular focus, elaborates upon what has already been stated in the seven maxims.

CHAPTER 2
The Effects of Incarceration

Now that we have looked at the justifications and the pious hopes for penitentiaries, and seen that they never change, let us turn to the effects of the institution. This is a subject which has had rather less publicity.

First, the *recidivist*.

It has been said, again and again, that the penitentiary is the ideal breeding ground for crime. In other words, the penitentiary encourages the very thing it is supposed to eliminate. Reports unanimously agree that, above all, the penal institution should protect society. Yet the very great majority of those who have been there once will go there again.

Exact figures on this phenomenon are difficult to obtain.

One may find the following in the study done by Abdel Fattah for the Law Reform Commission of Canada, *The Fear of Punishment*:

> "In most countries basic information about recidivism is not routinely collected, and there may thus be widespread misconceptions about the number of persons reconvicted. Even in the United States, statistics of the after-conduct of federal prisoners are not published."[14]

But the author adds:

> "Estimates of recidivism rates in countries where no official data is available vary from 50% to 80%."[15]

Unofficial estimates on the recidivism rate for federal penitentiaries have always been close to the maximum figure named by Fattah, that is, 80 per cent. The Penitentiary Commissioner tackled the problem from another angle during his testimony to the sub-committee, and in the process more or less corroborated this ball-park figure:

> "[In 1976] we had 28 per cent who had never been in jail before."[16]

Another important fact which affects the recidivism rate: we are imprisoning more and more people in Canada, and for longer periods of time. Once again, Fattah offers some interesting details:

> "A study by Taylor, at the Prison Department in England, found that three-year sentences of corrective training produced results which were slightly (though not significantly) *worse* than two-year sentences."[17]

In 1927, that is, more than fifty-five years ago, 2,000 of the 2,480 inmates in federal institutions were serving sentences of 2 to 8 years[18]. Even if it makes for a laborious comparison, let us take the year 1977, and note that in that year, when the number of inmates had reached 9,338, the average length of sentence had reached 7.3 years[19], and that some 700 prisoners were serving life sentences. We may thus make the following statement: the State knows that penitentiaries breed crime, yet it now imprisons more people, for longer periods of time. And the imposition of indeterminate sentences, as has already been seen in California, means that the period of time spent behind bars will lengthen.

As a sub-section of this topic of the effects of imprisonment, let us look at *the physical and psychological effects of such treatment.*

Here again, detailed studies are lacking. Indeed, the surprise would be to find they were *not* lacking. Knowing the unwillingness of the State to carry out proper studies on industrial illnesses, we would be naive to expect such initiative in an area where the State is trying to justify its policy. But even in the absence of detailed studies, it cannot be doubted that imprisonment, especially for a lengthy period of time, has disastrous effects upon the mind and body.

A recent study by the firm of industrial psychologists Pierre Dubois et Associés (1976) for the peace officers of the Public Service of Québec provided graphic evidence that the prison institution had extremely negative effects on prison guards.

Forty-two per cent of the group manifested stress symptoms on a regular or occasional basis, and the stress was directly linked to the danger, the rigours and the uncertainties of their work.

The report added that this nervous tension was manifested in physical as well as psychological ways, through such problems as gastric upsets, cardio-vascular troubles, nervous breakdowns, insomnia, and the like.

One can then project, from this report about guards, the physical degradation suffered by *inmates* in federal institutions. Given that these people must spend twenty-four hours of every day in the institution, that they receive scarcely any income at all, and that the stress is magnified by endless petty administrative irritations, by the arbitrary nature of the parole system and by harassment, one can easily imagine that the prisoner suffers ten times the stress levels of the guards.

The psychological repercussions of imprisonment have received somewhat more attention. Research to date has shown that an impoverished environment like a penitentiary, especially a maximum-security penitentiary, causes depression among its inmates. In fact, as soon as any individual receives reduced stimulation in their physical and social environment, they begin to suffer from serious emotional problems. The prisoner's environment is impoverished in the following ways:

a) restriction in the space available for movement when the prisoner feels a wish to move about;

b) restrictions in exchanges and verbal contact with other individuals when the prisoner wishes to communicate with cell-mates;

c) a routine that causes them to reject doing work well;

d) boredom caused by uniformity of food, dress and activities;

e) reduction in contact with things, with reality (which consists of diversity and variety);

f) the partial or total elimination of heterosexual relations, and a dependence on auto-sexuality and forced homosexuality;

g) reduction in hygiene and the quality of life.

This degradation, of course, is in addition to whatever physical ailments they may already suffer from, and the frequent accidents resulting from the prison environment: work, cruelty, self-mutilation.

The enormous lack of care of any kind obviously does nothing to protect the inmate's health. In 1971, for a total population of 7,458 inmates, the entire Canadian Penitentiary Service had only 23 doctors, 20 dentists, 23 psychiatrists and some 30 psychologists. The situation has scarcely improved since then. Some may argue that the doctor: inmate ratio is better than the doctor: patient ratio for Canadians as a whole (13:10,000 in 1971) or for Québécois (16:10,000 in 1974). But make no mistake: the slight edge in the numbers of specialists available in prison is more than nullified by the very limited access that prisoners in fact have to them, given the web of administrative obstacles, the lack of equipment in the institutions and all the other procedural difficulties in which they are caught.

A third effect of incarceration: *the increase in violence.*

The imprisonment of people who have shown themselves incapable (for various reasons) of living in harmony with their fellow beings has two effects. It increases the prisoner's difficulty in getting along with others, and it increases the aggressivity that is often inherent in the original crime. The depressed state so common to prisoners often turns into aggression as soon as the inmate is put into closer contact with the rest of the institution's population (following isolation) or with the community at large (following parole or liberation).

This aggression often takes one of two forms: violence against prison staff (primarily through hostage-takings) and other outward acts, and suicide.

The last six years have seen 57 hostage-taking incidents in Canadian penitentiaries, involving 161 inmates and 135 hostages. It is worth noting that no hostage has ever suffered serious harm at the hands of the inmates. It is even more worthy of note that 9 of the 12 hostage-takings in British Columbia during recent years occurred because the inmates wanted access to psychiatric care.

Although the setting itself strongly encourages these explosions, it is above all the stubbornness of the authorities that accounts for the recourse to violent action.

There have always been riots in Canadian penitentiaries. The years 1868, 1869, 1873, 1878, 1886, 1910, 1919, 1921, 1923, 1924, 1927, 1931, 1932, 1933, 1954, 1955, 1958, 1962, 1971, 1973, 1976 and 1977 have all been inscribed in flaming letters in the annuals of the Canadian Penitentiary Service. What they trace is an evolution from acts of individual rebellion to ones of collective grievances, accompanied by the destruction of walls and washstands. One should add that these outbursts of rage, accompanied by demands for prison improvements, reflect the social climate to be found outside the institutions, which itself has hardly been a model of peaceful calm.

A word here about prison escapes—which never pass unnoticed by the media, and which are yet another expression of the individual's aggression against prison environment. The point is, there are very few escapes—the average is one every seven years from maximum-security institutions. And, generally speaking, the number is declining all the time, as the result of extreme security measures: 186 in 1972, 115 in 1973, and 83 in 1974.

Now let us turn to the phenomenon of suicide, suicide being an act of aggression by the prisoners directed against themselves. The figures in Table I speak for themselves:

TABLE I
Suicides in Canadian Penitentiaries

Year	No. of Suicides	+Suicide Rate	+Suicide Rate in Canada
1960	3	47.3	7.6
1961	6	89.0	7.5
1962	1	14.0	7.2
1963	1	13.9	7.6
1964	4	52.3	8.2
1965	6	79.9	8.7
1966	10	134.4	8.6
1967	11	153.5	9.0
1968	16	227.7	9.8
1969	5	69.8	10.9
1970	19	267.3	11.3
1971	7	93.5	11.9
1972	7	84.8	12.2
1973	11	120.7	12.6
1974	7	82.4	12.9

+ Per 100,000 people

Source: Division of Statistics, Solicitor-General of Canada

In other words, between 1960 and 1974, 108 prisoners took their lives. This is ten times the suicide rate for Canadians as a whole.

And as Professor Denis Szabo declares (a man hardly to be suspected of leftist theories): "What surprises me is that there are not more suicides. Prison is an artificial environment, and not adequate to the needs of mental health."[20]

The judicial system has been asked to pass judgment on this appalling situation, but has yet to condemn the prison system.

A few cases, selected from many:

- On May 14, 1965, Jean-Guy Généreux hanged himself with a sheet reinforced with a steel wire in his cell in St. Vincent de Paul. The official conclusion: "Violent death without criminal responsibility."

- On June 3, 1966, Sylvio Turner hanged himself from the bars of his cell in St. Vincent de Paul. The authorities held an inquiry to determine whether or not there had been negligence on the part of prison personnel. No follow-up. Naturally.

- On June 13, 1966, Gérard Duclos, aged 21, killed himself in St. Vincent de Paul. Listen to the testimony given by correctional officer Marcel Lafrenière to the coroner's inquiry: "Duclos was of a steady and secretive nature. He spoke to officials only when it was strictly necessary. But he was cracking jokes with other inmates the day he hanged himself..." Coroner Lapointe suggested to the jurors that there was "evidence of suicide." They instead opted for a decision of "violent death by suicide in a moment of nervous or mental depression without any criminal responsibility."

- On January 19, 1967, David McDowell hanged himself in the Leclerc Institute and prisoner Dezainde hanged himself in St. Vincent de Paul. Witness Léo Flynn, assistant-director at St. Vincent de Paul, testified in the Dezainde case: "... the inmate had recently been returned to a regular cell after having broken up several cells in the psychiatric wing where he was receiving intensive treatment." Under the worthy guidance of Mr. Laurier Lapointe, the jury delivered two verdicts of suicide.

- On March 16, 1967, Aurèle Rozon, 20 years of age, hanged himself in the "hole," the isolation wing, of St. Vincent de Paul. Once again, guided by Mr. Lapointe, the jury brought in a verdict of suicide.

- On July 25, 1968, Georges Provencher hanged himself in St. Vincent de Paul. Same verdict.

- On February 16, 1970, Michael Calahan, 18 years of age, was found hanged in his cell in St. Vincent de Paul. He had been imprisoned the day after being sentenced to two years for "attempted assault and battery with intention of theft." Same verdict of suicide.

The list could continue indefinitely. With the same verdicts.

Let us conclude by noting that the suicide rate is particularly high in maximum-security institutions, with a rate of ten deaths every three years for each of these establishments.[21]

There is not enough information available to make a table of self-mutilations in penitentiaries. But we can state that it must be extremely high, given the suicide rate. Let us simply point out that for every successful suicide in the former Special Correctional Unit of the Laval penitentiary complex, there were roughly 43 attempts. A parallel may be drawn for other establishments.

The final aspect to be considered among the effects of imprisonment, *the violation of the inmate's rights.*

Even though a prison sentence legally orders only the restriction of the guilty party's liberty, they are in fact stripped of virtually all their rights. The reason is that the criteria guiding the institution in which they are imprisoned function in such a way that rights are contemptuously ignored. This was noted by the Criminal Lawyers Association of Ontario in their submission to the McGuigan sub-committee:

> "The Canadian Penitentiary Service regards the civil rights of a person who is sentenced to a period of incarceration as being virtually extinguished."[22]

The only rights, or rather, privileges, are those which are explicitly recognized in penal policy, as laid down by the Commissioner's instructions and the requirements of the Penitentiary Act. And this is the ruling principle for even the most trivial of daily routines: disciplinary questions within the institutions, transfers to other institutions, and parole.

It creates a curious paradox within the penitentiary: supposedly created to enforce respect for bourgeois justice among those who have supposedly flouted it, the penitentiary in fact deprives its prisoners of societal norms and forces them to live in a world of the arbitrary and the dictatorial.

Violation of Political Rights

First, the electoral law strips the 9300 people in federal penitentiaries of their right to vote. The most elementary notion of justice, however, would insist that those who are subjected to a policy have the right to make known their opinion on the subject.

The same kind of repression extends to the right to parole, and the rights of association, of assembly and of the press.

The Canadian Penitentiary Service explicitly withdraws these rights (guaranteed by the Canadian Bill of Rights) because the directives of the Commissioner, allegedly for security reasons, insists that they be controlled and restrained (not to mention eliminated).

Violation of Judicial Rights

Canadians as a whole have a right to a trial before an independent judge according to the requirements of natural justice, and to a defence benefiting from all the prerogatives of positive rights. The situation for the prisoner is entirely different.

In all matters of internal discipline, the prisoner/accused has no right to legal counsel and no right to call witnesses (cf., the part of the Instructions dealing with the hearings of accusations and procedure). Instead, the prisoner receives a sham hearing which confirms the total domination of the accused by the authorities. Any semblance of justice in this process depends entirely on the officer who happens to preside at the hearing.

If the words of the regional director, J.M. Murphy of the Canadian Penitentiary Service, are to be believed, this is the appropriate situation:

> "As Regional Director I feel there is no place for any lawyer in an institution."[23]

His opinion is shared by the directors as a group.

Finally, to come back to the way in which judgment is pronounced in these questions of internal discipline, no minutes are taken at the hearing, justice is "summary" indeed, and the reasons for the decision are not made known. It is difficult, in this matter as in others, to obtain information from the Canadian Penitentiary Service about these administrative procedures and their arbitrary nature.

In his study, *Crimes et châtiments au Canada français,** Raymond Boyer reproduced statistics on the verdicts pronounced in St. Vincent de Paul during the 1930s.

TABLE II[24]
Judgments passed on infractions in
St. Vincent de Paul

	1930-31	1931-32	1932-33	1933-34	1934-35	1935-36
Infractions	1,961	2,753	2,267	1,615	1,967	1,537
Acquittals	17	13	3	1	—	—
Reprieves	38	19	46	17	44	24

That is, of the 12,100 infractions to be judged in the St. Vincent de Paul Penitentiary during a six-year period, there were 34 (0.28%) acquittals and 188 (1.5%) reprieves.

The situation has hardly changed in the intervening forty years. As the study group on dissociation (Vantour) reported in 1975, during a three-month period there were 975 verdicts rendered by disciplinary committees in seven establishments. Six acquittals took place—0.62% of the cases heard!

Caught in that kind of a trap, the prisoners theoretically have three possible lines of redress. One, they can send a petition to the Commissioner; two, they can use internal grievance procedures. But in both cases, they must work through the Canadian Penitentiary Service, which is the very

---

* *Crime and Punishment in French Canada*—translator's note.

41

organization about which they are complaining. The third avenue is to appeal to the ombudsman. But the ombudsman may only make recommendations, and his position is authorized by the solicitor-general...

Of course, the prisoner can also contact an independent lawyer. But a lawyer may only make an informal inquiry into the pertinence of the disciplinary procedures, since to date the courts have refused to hear any appeals.

And if, somehow, the prisoner does manage to appeal to an outside court, the judge of that court, as a general rule, has no authority. One interesting example is furnished by the case of Gilles Hébert, accused of having killed prison guard Paul Gosselin during an escape from hospital. Recaptured and imprisoned once again, the prisoner appeared in court. This is how the hearing went:

Defence lawyer:	They threw him [Gilles Hébert] in the hole, they gassed him, they cut off the water so that he couldn't ease his discomfort with a damp facecloth. He was deprived of sleep and had pepper put in his coffee. He was systematically prevented from sleeping.
Lawyer for the Crown: Me. Lerous	The presumption of innocence also holds for jail wardens. And they must have the opportunity to justify themselves.
Judge Lessard:	As this is an administrative matter, I can do no more than recommend that the prisoner be transferred to another institution.[25]

Administrative isolation — "to maintain good order and discipline in the institution" — by virtue of paragraph 230 of the Regulations of the Canadian Penitentiary Service, may be applied to anyone at the discretion of the administration. And once again, without any true defence being possible against the measure. Facts show that it is usually ordered for one of two reasons: one, as an act of vengeance; the other, as an effort to disrupt attempts at prisoner organization. One good example was the isolation ordered for four prisoner delegates following a press conference held at the Correctional Development Centre in February, 1977.

The consequences are often dramatic — as in the case of Bob Landers, who died in isolation in Millhaven Institute in Ontario, from lack of care following a heart attack.

When the director of Millhaven was called upon to testify at the inquiry, he stated the punishment had been ordered so as to prevent the victim from promoting prisoners' rights and organizing (without violence) a prisoners committee.

Instances of prisoner transfer show the same tendencies.

The choice of institution can be of great importance to the prisoner. But, once again, the decision is left up to the penitentiary administration and subject to no outside judicial control.

The same realities apply to parole.

The date of prisoners' liberation depends on a number of factors outside their control. According to the present law and to the one recently passed, the Parole Commission is not required to conduct a hearing with the prisoner in order to rule whether or not there is a right to parole. Consequently, inappropriate, erroneous and irrelevant information can accumulate in the prisoner's dossier and go unchallenged. The abuses are flagrant. And, very frequently, deliberate falsification is carried out so as to prejudice the prisoner's chances for parole.

With the abolition of the statutory reduction of sentences and the institution of merit reductions, the discretionary powers of the administration are increased.

Finally, even if the prisoner receives parole, the ex-prisoner is always threatened by the possibility of its suspension or revocation. Once again, the Commission is not required to tell the prisoner the reasons for the suspension and/or revocation of parole.

Violation of Fundamental Economic Rights

Work is done in penitentiaries. But its major purpose is to help stabilize the penitentiary structure. Thus, the prisoners are obliged to work (whenever they are not being forced to spend 23 hours a day in their cells), and receive very poor wages for work done — 75 cents to $1.20 a day, of which about one-third is put into forced savings. Moreover, coercion is widely applied, for the prisoner who refuses to work when he ought to co-operate is challenging not only the value of specific work programmes, but the general authority of the prison administration as well.

The Canadian government recognizes that all people — except prisoners — have the right to choose their work and to receive a reasonable wage for it. A whole series of legislative measures require industrial activities to respect elementary social norms. Despite obvious weaknesses, the minimum-wage law and social policies like unemployment insurance do guarantee the population a certain level of income. Except for prisoners, that is, who find themselves deprived of such rights. (And as far as the right to form a union goes, it is obviously not tolerated at all — for, "security" reasons.)

Present work programmes have two objectives:

1. the maintenace of prison installations; and
2. the accomplishment of work which benefits the Canadian government, such as the manufacture and repair of mail bags. Eventually, also, the construction of metal furniture.

Canadian Penitentiary Service policy requires that the prisoner carry out a full day's work, and that he forego social benefits. That is the extent of guidance on working conditions. Any refusal by prisoners to work is considered an infraction, which will result in the loss of statutory reduction of the sentence, isolation in their cells and a general loss of privileges.

CHAPTER 3
The Prisoners' Reaction

Having given a summary review of the effects of incarceration, it is now time to examine the reaction of the prisoner confronted with this kind of reality. Or, to put it another way, how a person reacts when they are spied upon by guards, when they cannot choose their friends, when their letters and other writings are censored, when their conversations are listened to, when their personal space is reduced to the absolute minimum, when the occupation of their time is regulated and checked off for every moment of the 24 hours in a day, when they are refused certain visitors, lose contact with family and friends and their own identity, when their dress is regimented, when they are not free to get up, move about, eat, or take a shower when they wish, when they have almost no personal belongings, when their salary is almost non-existent, their occupations tedious, their entire life programme decided by others, when they lose their right to heterosexual relations and are forced to resort to masturbation and/or homosexuality and when, on top of all that, they suffer the daily provocation, domination and harassment of armed men and the snail-like pace of a bureaucracy which can take months to give permission for the slightest trifle.

The accumulated restrictions imposed upon the movements and wishes of the prisoner prevent the satisfaction of the most elementary needs for a normal life. And the prisoner is hit by this situation from the first moment he/she steps behind bars.

In general, one may state that the prisoners who neither kill themselves nor fall into the small minority that adjusts to prison life will emerge from prison very different persons than they were when they went in. This generalization holds true, no matter how long they have stayed behind bars, or what kind of institution they were in.

In order to understand the pattern of adaptation to the prison milieu, we must refer to the studies carried out by Goffman. In his work, *Asiles*, he says that the penitentiary is a totalitarian institution. He defines it in this way:

> "A place of residence and of work where a large number of individuals are placed in the same situation, cut off from the exterior world for a relatively long period of time, and are leading the life of a recluse whose modalities are relatively regulated."[26]

Another author shares Goffman's opinion of maximum-security institutions. In an article which appeared in *The Criminal Journal of Criminology and Correction*, entitled "A Miniature Totalitarian State Maximum Security Prison," Henry Burns compares the penitentiary system to a dictatorial system under six headings:

1. The ideology which defines the inmate is exclusively the creation of those who hold power in the institution.
2. Discipline, regulations and their application belong solely to the authorities, and may not be questioned.
3. Force and brutality are used to enforce the regulations.
4. The circulation of information into and out of the prison environment is entirely under the control of the administration.
5. The total concentration of arms, and thus of force, is in the hands of the administration and its

personnel.

6. Extreme bureaucratization and concentration of economic power are obvious.

The objectives and the justifications for such institutions are also accurately described: they are

"intended to protect the community against supposedly deliberate attack, not to make the interests of the prisoners their major objective."[27]

A certain number of prisoner reactions — to be precise, four — are possible. The first is *"withdrawal,* whereby the inmate apparently ceases to pay any attention to anything that does not happen in his immediate presence. This radical refusal of all personal participation in interfering events is known by the name of regression, of psychosis, in prisons."[28]

Next comes *"the path of intransigence,"* whereby "the inmate issues a voluntary challenge to the institution by openly refusing to co-operate with its personnel."[29]

There is also *"installation."* This is "well known to penitentiary personnel when they say of someone that he is institutionalized. The inmate builds up a stable and relatively satisfying existence by gathering all the satisfactions he can find in the institution."[30]

Finally, there is *"conversion,"* in which "the prisoner seems to adopt the attitudes of the administration and tries to play the role of the model inmate. The convert adopts a more submissive, rigid, neutral attitude, presenting the image of a person who in all circumstances reflects back to staff members his enthusiasm for the institution."[31]

The penitentiary institution, in turn, reacts to each of these four strategies. The classification officer or the psychologist chooses a new approach, or extends the present one. The goal is always the same: to shake the inmates out of a situation which, by increasing their sense of security, renders them less vulnerable to repression.

Therefore, the persons who have a tendency to withdraw into themselves are required to take part in various activities, to "carry out projects." The stubborn individuals are met with even more stubborn efforts to break their wills. The prisoners who are at peace within the institution are

47

tempted with visions of the outside world, so as to alienate them from the prison environment. Finally, the apparently "rehabilitated" prisoners are forced to compromise themselves to an ever-greater extent, to ensure that they will be forever marked by their prison experience. Punishment, thus, is to be internalized. Though the prison doors will one day open, the ex-prisoners will drag their cells and their guards around with them to the end of their days.

Perhaps the most mystifying thing about this process of annihilation, which will be examined in the next section, is that the authorities see the penitentiary institution as an eternal verity, outside history, without beginning or evolution, and isolated from the march of events. That which has no beginning, no history, cannot have an end. The battle for the abolition of prisons, therefore, logically makes no sense, since according to this mythology, prisons are with us for all eternity!

This perspective tends to cut off the penitentiary institution from its historic roots and is, of course, reinforced by the zeal with which authorities at all levels centre the entire process on the criminal and crime. The prisoners are not workers; they are criminals. Their crimes have deprived them of all class membership. In the same way, the institution in which they are confined has no political rationale, and no history. It is just a building which has been constructed in order to protect "society," is governed according to certain regulations and is administered by its responsible authorities.

True enough, one sometimes hears vague reports to the effect that the penitentiaries have put an end to corporal punishment, that they have humanized sentences, that there were some Quakers behind those measures and that conditions are better now than in the past. But nothing more precise than that.

The authorities make sure that the prisoners have as little contact as possible with reality — their purpose being, of course, to head off a rising tide of organization, of challenge, or of conscious struggle.

In order to destroy this myth of the a-historicity (i.e., of existence outside history) of penitentiaries, the following two chapters will briefly present the history of the penitentiary institution in the world as a whole, and in Canada.

After sketching the institution's history, it will be easier to discern its political rationale.

PART TWO:
The Historical Link

Photo Credit: Canada Wide. St.Vincent de Paul (1948).

CHAPTER 1
The History of Penitentiaries

And so we have seen that the basic contradiction between the reality of imprisonment (injustice and violence) and the principle which gave rise to it and which is still used to justify it ("justice and the protection of society"), cannot be resolved. There is nothing temporary about this contradiction; it is inherent in the institution itself.

We have also seen that the people who must submit to such oppression adapt to it with a variety of mechanisms which include both rebellion and the belief that their situation cannot be logically explained or defended.

Studying the history of penitentiaries allows us to put individual experiences into their collective context.

It is important to distinguish between the general term "prison" and the specific institution of the "penitentiary." According to the *Oxford Dictionary*, a prison is a "place in which [a] person is kept in capitivity." It is undoubtedly as old as the history of human conflict, and includes within this definition such things as the hole, the cage, the dungeon — in other words, any place where a captive may be confined. The term "penitentiary," however, implies treatment for the person under detention. That is the distinguishing characteristic of the institution.

Oxford defines "penitentiary" as "Of penance; of reformatory treatment." The historical growth of this notion may be traced. Our present penitentiaries are the direct descendants of the correctional system first devised by the Roman Catholic Church a good thousand years ago. Even if the immediate origins of the "science" of penology lie in the 17th century and the applications of that science in the 19th century, canon law had long since taught that anti-social behaviour was a sin and that the sinner must be returned, through segregation and penitence, to the path of righteousness.

The Catholic Church

In 817, the Council of Aix-la-Chapelle instituted a cellular system of imprisonment, and recommended that those being detained in the cells be provided with books, regular visits and work.

This régime, which was subsequently modified and refined, was applied by the Church to those individuals in its various institutions who deviated from the Rule.

In 1266, the Council of Bézier ruled that people sentenced to this régime by ecclesiastical authorities were to be isolated by night, but given communal exercise, in strict silence, by day.

Christian charity had its place within the system: prison visits were identified as one of the seven works of the Misericord.

The Monk Mabillon (1632-1797)

Despite the teachings and example of the Church, however, lay society long resisted any modification to its methods of dealing with criminals. The most frequent punishments continued to be public forms of torture such as the wheel, various kinds of mutilation, banishment and being sent to the galleys. But in 1690, a Benedictine monk named Mabillon produced a document called, *Réflexions sur les* *prisons des ordres religieux.** It was the first effort to extend to the lay sphere precepts which, until then, had been applied solely within religious institutions. It was also the first gropings toward a "science" of penology.

The monk opposed absolute isolation for prisoners, and proposed a number of reforms in the areas of hygiene, ventilation, visits and work to be done by the prisoners. He even included a sketch of the physical layout of the ideal prison.

Mabillon also observed that the same sentence would have a different impact on different persons, depending on their individual temperaments. He therefore recommended that both the length of the sentence and the way in which it was to be enforced be adapted to each prisoner.

His book led to the establishment of several model institutions in a number of European Catholic states. Italy took the lead: San Michele, founded by Pope Clement XI, opened in Rome in 1703, followed by prisons in Turin (1757), Milan (1759) and Venice (1760). Each was equipped with individual cells, and with special quarters for women and children.

The Protestant Reply: the Rasphuis

A similar movement was astir in the countries of the Protestant Reformation. The Rasphuis (the men's prison in Amsterdam), which opened in 1596, applied some of the principles being advocated by the Roman Catholic Church, and inspired a number of similar institutions in other Protestant states. The Rasphuis provided the historical link between the dominant theory of the 16th century—that of the spiritual, pedagogic transformation of the individual—and the new penitentiary model which was to take shape in the second half of the 18th century.

The Rasphuis was organized according to three main principles:

---

* *Reflections on the Prisons of Religious Orders*—transl. note

1. Obligatory work performed in congregate;
2. Solitary confinement for punishment purposes only — normally, inmates slept two or three to a bed in a room which held four to twelve people; and
3. Discretionary powers (within certain limits) for the prison administration itself to determine the length of the sentence to be served, according to the behaviour of the prisoner in question.

Prisoners were paid for their labour. The main principles of the system were fleshed out with an elaborate network of policies — the relentless occupation of every instant of the prisoner's day, a complex system of prohibitions and obligations, and constant surveillance, exhortations and spiritual counselling, all designed to "attract toward the good" and "turn away from evil."

There was strong criticism of the Rasphuis model: severe overcrowding sharply reduced the prisoner's chances for moral improvement and increased their opportunities for conspiracy and rebellion.

The Pedagogy of Work: the Ghent prison, Belgium

In 1773, Jean Jacques Philippe Vilain XIV, grand bailiff of the State of Flanders, published his *Mémoire sur les moyens de corriger les malfaiteurs.** It inspired the direction taken by the new prison in Ghent, which turned out to be another experiment in the infant science of penology.

The originality of the Ghent prison was its attempt to make penal labour economically profitable for the State. Labour, of course, was essential, for it was assumed at the time that the major cause of crime was idleness. The Ghent prison foresaw two major beneficial results from its approach:

1. It would reduce that great burden to the State, the cost of criminal activity; and

---

* *Notes on the Means of Correcting Evil-Doers* — transl. note

2. It would provide a large number of new workers, thereby (through competition) driving down the cost of labour.

Work, therefore, was obligatory at Ghent. And since it was remunerated, the prisoner could be given better treatment both during and after imprisonment. The length of sentence to be served varied according to two factors: the possibility of correcting the individual concerned, and the prisoner's economic usefulness.

Ghent evolved beyond the Rasphuis model in that it attempted to turn a profit on the work done by its prisoners. Prisons transformed themselves, at least in part, into cheap-labour factories.

John Howard (1726-1790) and the Gloucester Model

In 1777, John Howard published the results of his observations of the world's prisons. He argued for good food for the prisoners and good ventilation in their quarters, for considerable but not absolute isolation of each prisoner, and for a system based on meaningful work and careful spiritual formation.

Howard's role in the evolution of penitentiaries may be compared to that of the Italian jurist and his contemporary, Beccaria, in penal law: both men opposed the use of torture and excessive punishment, and recommended the imposition of sentences based instead on the need to protect society.

The prison built at Gloucester was to determine the English model. Hanway, a reformer along Howard's own lines, devised its system. He too argued for isolation of the prisoners, on the grounds that crowding prisoners together not only allowed the worst among them to influence the others, but provided opportunities for conspiracies and escapes. He criticized the Ghent prison (among others), saying that it too closely resembled a mass-labour factory.

Hanway felt that the "terrible shock" of solitary confinement, by isolating the prisoners from evil influences and forcing them back on their own thoughts, was the starting-point for the prisoner's discovery of their conscience and the "path of righteousness." Solitary labour, therefore, was as much an exercise in spiritual transformation as an apprenticeship to a trade.

With Gloucester, the concept of deprivation of liberty as a means of reform appeared in civil law for the first time.

The separate cell, therefore—which Hanway called a "reformatory"—was to be the site for, and the means of, the transformation of the individual, thereby restoring to the state subjects who had been lost to it. At Gloucester, the most dangerous criminals lived in continual solitary confinement. The others worked in common (making rope and bags, polishing marble, etc.) but were isolated in their separate cells at night.

Impact of the French Revolution (1789) on Penitentiaries

The French Revolution marked the end of the Ancien Régime and the seizure of power by the bourgeoisie. The Constituent Assembly of 1791 carried out a far-reaching reform of the penal code, making deprivation of liberty the new basis for the system of repression. However, the near-abolition of corporal punishment (whippings and a wide variety of tortures) should not be interpreted as a humanitarian gesture: it was only a change in the purpose of punishment. The triumphant bourgeoisie, the class now in power, made changes in the law and penalties in order to make punishment a more effective guarantor of social and political stability.

The fall of the monarchy had taught its lessons: punishment was to be less visible, and more profitable.

Terror is indispensable to power but, very cleverly, the bourgeoisie rejected the highly visible terror of the Ancien Régime (with its public hangmen in the town square) in favour of systematized fear.

The system was to be the penitentiary.

Judges acquired a new vocabulary: they no longer talked of punishing the guilty but, instead, of correcting, rehabilitating and "curing" them.

The role of the penal administration would be to carry out the sentences pronounced in court. Offences were to be codified. Justice would no longer be proclaimed in the name of the king, but in the name of society. The bourgeoisie would not moralize directly; it would wield power and justify oppression indirectly, camouflaging it under the notion of the common good.

The haphazard innovations of previous centuries in the concept of penitentiaries would be systematically codified, and applied. The English philosopher Jeremy Bentham even provided the architectural model of the ideal penitentiary: it would be a circular "Penopticon," whose shape would allow authorities to keep all prisoners under surveillance at a glance.

The penitentiary code took shape:

1. Elimination of the criminal: as long as the guilty party was in prison, there was no danger of his committing new offences;
2. General prevention: others would be discouraged from taking up criminal activities themselves;
3. Individual intimidation: present suffering would lead to proper future behaviour;
4. Improvement: the individual would be corrected, transformed into a better person; and
5. Self-censorship: the certainty of punishment (rather than the disgusting spectacle of executions) would cause the individual to become his own disciplinarian.

However, the troubled period of revolution and Empire prevented the application in France of the desired changes to the system.

Their application fell instead to a country on the other side of the Atlantic.

The United States and the Birth of the Modern Penitentiary System

In 1776, the United States gained independence, and the bourgeoisie gained power. Independence was followed by a period of serious economic decline, and the new authorities had to cope with a sharp increase in criminal activities. The Quakers of Pennsylvania and of West Jersey, with their own long experience as victims of repression, pushed for some substitute for corporal punishment.

Just as in France, the new dominant class in the United States saw that revision of the criminal code could help make the exercise of power more efficient. It would also be a subtle means of guaranteeing the stability of a régime facing the threat of popular uprisings. The first reforms were made in the State of Pennsylvania: in 1794, it abolished the death sentence for all crimes except first-degree murder, and replaced corporal punishment with imprisonment.

By the Acts of 1789, 1790 and 1794, the Walnut Street prison was converted into a state prison and new buildings, containing blocks of cells, were added. This was the start of the first of the two models of penitentiary organization which were to influence the entire world.

The Pennsylvania System

The construction in 1829 of the Cherry Hill penitentiary in Philadelphia was the beginning of the "Pennsylvania system." Cherry Hill took its inspiration from the Ghent and Gloucester models: the institution was to be self-sufficient thanks to obligatory prison labour. Inmates were paid for the work they did, on the assumption that this would assure their moral and material reintegration into society upon release. Prisoners condemned to death lived in solitary confinement; otherwise, solitary was used only as a means of special punishment. The prisoner's behaviour influenced the length of his imprisonment. Sentences were not to be made public knowledge, and if the sentence did become known, it was still carried out in secret. As elsewhere, Bibles and other religious

60

books were provided to prisoners as an instrument of behaviour modification. A file was maintained on each prisoner, and city officials came regularly to read through the files. Prisoners were divided into four broad categories:

1. those condemned to solitary confinement for serious offences;
2. dangerous delinquents and recidivists;
3. occasional delinquents; and
4. first offenders.

The system had a clear orientation: the purpose of the sentence was to prevent future crime, individual variations of sentence were permitted. The Pennsylvania system corrected the abuses, noted and deplored elsewhere, of crowded, congregate living. However, a cellular prison (such as Cherry Hill) was more expensive to build, and work within it more difficult to organize than in the old congregate prisons. Moreover, the cellular model provoked mental disorders, despair and suicide among the inmates.

Slowly, this system of imprisonment was dropped, being retained only in detention centres and in institutions for those serving short sentences. This change, however, did not come without a struggle.

The Auburn System

The "Auburn model"—a combination of aspects of both the congregate system of imprisonment and the cellular one—was first tried in the United States in 1816, in the Auburn prison of the State of New York. Under this programme, prisoners slept each in their own cell but were together during the day. In this way, promiscuity was very greatly reduced, yet the dangers of isolation were largely avoided. Silence was mandatory, and the kind of industrial production encouraged under this régime seems to have been more efficient than that of the Pennsylvania model.

Proponents of each system waged bitter polemical warfare for many years, with the Prison Discipline Society of Boston (which favoured the Auburn system) pitted against the

Philadelphia Society for Alleviating the Miseries of Public Prisons (which favoured the Pennsylvania system).

The turning point came in 1845, when the influential Prison Society of New York sided with the Boston group and thus with the Auburn model. The Pennsylvania model was finally dropped by every one of the prisons which had earlier adopted it. For example, Maryland, which had adopted the cellular model in 1809, abandoned it in 1838. Massachusetts, which had adopted it in 1811, abandoned it in 1829. Maine's experiment with solitary confinement lasted only from 1824 to 1827; Virginia's from 1824 to 1833; Rhode Island's from 1838 to 1844. When New Jersey dropped the Pennsylvania model in 1858, the change-over was complete.

Europe Investigates and Chooses the Pennsylvania Model

The Restoration in France was an age of social stability. The authorities initiated a number of studies of the American reforms so as to be in a position to establish a rationally-based penitentiary system throughout the country. The pioneer effort took place in Chaptal, which as early as 1801 began to gather information about the American experiments. Next, Descazes (1819) and Villermé (1820) visited the United States itself in order to carry out their research. In 1819, Louis XVIII founded the Superior Council of Prisons, which set to work on a huge study of its own. And then, in 1830, a major step was taken when the Chamber of Paris asked the government to begin the job of prison reform.

And so G. de Beaumont (1802-1866) and Alexis de Tocqueville (1805-1859) visited the United States, first in 1831 and again jn 1836. In 1836, they offered their conclusions in a document entitled *Le système pénitentiaire aux États-Unis.**
It favoured the Pennsylvania model. Demetz and Blouet made the same trip in 1835, and came to the same conclusions.

England sent over Sir W. Crawford in 1834. His *Report*

---

* *The Penitentiary System of the United States* —transl. note

on the Penitentiaries of the United States agreed with the French authors: the Pennsylvania model was best.

Dr. Nicolaus H. Julius studied the Pennsylvania system on behalf of the Prussian authorities, and went home highly enthusiastic about what he had seen.

And so, the Pennsylvania model was widely adopted in Europe: in England in 1835; Belgium, 1838; Sweden, 1840; Denmark, 1846; Norway, 1851; and Holland, 1851. In France, the first steps in this direction were taken at Petite Roquette, where cellular imprisonment was instituted, but the trend began to reverse itself after the Haussonville studies towards 1875.

European Innovations: the Irish system, open prisons...

Although the Pennsylvania system received wide acceptance in Europe during the first half of the 19th century, different countries introduced a number of modifications which at least mitigated the system, though they did not contradict its basic principles. A Frenchman named H. de Neuville came up with the concept of a progressive system which was first applied by an Englishman, Captain Maconochie, in Australia in 1840, and later introduced to Ireland by Walter Crofton. This "Irish Progressive System," as it came to be called, in effect combined two earlier models: a prisoner began sentence under the cellular system (Pennsylvania) but later "progressed" to a system of congregate labour by day (Auburn). During this second phase, good conduct and signs of rehabilitation won the prisoner "marks" toward a series of privileges including tickets of leave and parole.

The Irish system provided for individualized sentences, wages for the best of the prisoners and constant encouragement for all. However, it also caused certain difficulties in the organization of work, and was criticized for encouraging prisoners to "play the game" in hypocritical fashion.

In 1846, Bonneville de Marsongy drew up a parole scheme which was essentially a further modification on the Irish Progressive model.

During the second half of the 19th century, Montessinor in Spain and Obermaies in Bavaria both experimented with schooling and job-training in their prisons.

In 1891, the Swiss instituted the first open prison, the agricultural colony of Witzwill. It was developed by Otto Kellerhols, who made a radical break with the traditional closed systems by having the prisoners work out of doors. Until then — except in the final stages of the Irish Progressive System — all prisoners were always shut away in closed buildings. In this Swiss experiment, however, there were no bars, no walls. The model (which attracted few imitators) had the advantage of putting the prisoner in a situation closely resembling life in normal society, since it had him working outside and permitted the evolution from prisoner to free person.

"Softening" of the System in the United States

A second wave of prison construction took place in the United States from 1850 to 1920. The growing industrialization of the country and the massive immigration to it combined to make more and more repression necessary.

However, the frequency of prison riots forced the authorities to rethink, to some extent, both the conditions of detention and the programmes for the prisoners. It was clear that simply depriving persons of their liberty did not automatically reform them.

Measures such as probation, parole and indeterminate sentences were all introduced. Somewhat paradoxically, the State quite readily adopted the first two innovations, but baulked at the third. California, for example, introduced parole in 1893-94 but waited another 23 years to impose the abominable system of indeterminate sentences. The other States followed much the same pattern.

Indeterminate sentences, mind you, had already been tried in the New York House of Refuge in the mid-1820s — though in a modified form, for the judge had to set the sentence somewhere between a pre-ordained maximum and minimum. Under the new measure, however, the penitentiary administration was given full discretion to set the sentence at anything from one year to perpetuity. It is ironic to note that it was precisely the people most anxious to "humanize" the system who caused it to adopt the worst horror of all.

As we have already seen, the 1860s brought a wave of prison "liberalization" in Europe. Innovations like job training, parole and the progressive system had caught the attention of American reformers like Dwight and Wines of the New York Prison Association, Brockway of the Detroit House of Correction, and Hubbon, director of Sing Sing Penitentiary in the State of New York.

The authorities yielded to their combined pressure, and approved, as a pilot project, the construction of an experimental institution at Elmira, New York. When the prison opened its doors in 1877, its first director was Brockway, one of the instigators of the whole project.

Policies developed at Elmira were to have enormous influence in the coming years. The whole issue of open-ended sentences was thoroughly debated at the Congress of Criminal Anthropology held in Paris in 1889. Many of its participants challenged a whole range of concepts of penal philosophy that had, until then, been unquestioningly received as dogma, and all of them agreed on what was then a revolutionary idea: the sentence should fit the individual. The logical extension of this idea, of course, was the indeterminate sentence.

Procedures were established, beyond either the provisions of the criminal code or the arbitary verdict of judges, to classify inmates, determine their sentences and administer their punishment. It seemed entirely logical that the length of the sentence should hinge on the behaviour of the prisoner. In all the excitement, however, it was "forgotten" that the institution would itself have a determining effect on the prisoner. A mere detail... After all, this attitude permitted them to go on tinkering for several more decades with a system that in fact cried out for a complete overhaul.

The most determined supporter for the system at the Congress in Paris, incidentally, was H.D. Wey, medical director at the Elmira Reformatory and Brockway's successor. Pilot projects are never without their consequences.

The Labour Issue

Until the end of the 19th century, prison labour was highly profitable for the State and for big business alike, but strongly opposed throughout the century by artisans and other small producers. The tiny pittance paid the prisoners guaranteed that their products could be sold at a price that undercut all competition. The authorities tried to win over opponents to the prison-labour system by putting—to some extent, anyway—the cheap manpower at their disposal as well. The best-known of these efforts was the establishment of an open-face iron mine near Pittsburgh, which ran on prison labour from 1844 to 1851. The idea was to supply local industries with raw materials, but once the mine was exhausted, the experiment came to an end.

Some authors claim that it was opposition by organized labour which led to the general abolition of large-scale production within penitentiaries. However, the study of union history in the United States at the time shows that it was in fact the bosses, not the unions, who put up the major resistance. Still, the whole question deserves further study.

The controversy came to an end in the middle of the century, when the State of New York introduced a policy guaranteeing that the products of prison labour would no longer be allowed to compete on the open market. This legislation had a restraining influence on the practices being followed by the other States.

The Human Sciences Make Their Appearance

The need to individualize sentences attracted psychologists to the study of the field of imprisonment in general. Around 1906, men like William James, G. Stanley Hall, Adolf Meyer and their students, H.H. Goddard and William Healy, all of them standard-bearers in the "Boston group" for the new psychology, began formulating a number of measures intended to improve the penitentiary system.

The goal of these measures was to transform penitentiaries into something more closely resembling treatment centres. There had already been a number of experiments with this idea, notably at Utica State Asylum in New York in 1834 and in Dannemore at the turn of the century, but never in the systematic fashion now being proposed by the Boston group.

William Healey was the most influential of them all, since he was the first to take action: he opened a clinic for delinquents in Chicago in 1909. The significance of such initiatives for the prison scene as a whole was that they introduced the idea that the criminal was a patient, who required treatment. At the same time, intensive psychiatric research was begun on the whole question of a scientific classification system for prisoners, according to psychological type. These were the first efforts to standardize procedures which until then had been left to the individual discretion of each prison administration. The pioneers in this area were Doctors Thomas W. Salmon and Bernard Glueck, of the Sing Sing psychiatric clinic.

Prison therapy programmes came to be modelled almost exclusively on the group-therapy approach championed by the English psychologist Jones. This approach rested on two main assumptions:

1. The (assumed) near-inability of the prisoners to communicate with others, to understand the feelings of others and to express themselves (noted by Fréchette in 1970); and

2. The observed difficulty experienced by psychopaths in taking on societal roles. It was noted that the more delinquent the individuals, the more trouble they have assuming these roles.

Group therapy was being promoted as the way to cure the "criminal" patient, through the use of such techniques as psychodrama (role-playing to explore the emotional state of the participants), Gestalt therapy (the interaction of the human organism with his environment) and the bio-energetic technique (which worked on the assumption that muscular tension was a key factor in emotional disturbance).

The Therapeutic Community took some measures along these lines in the 1930s for repeated and/or dangerous offenders, and by 1950 some forty institutions in the United States had similar programmes. In the 1960s, the approach swept the world, and was adopted by institutions such as the Van der Haevan Clinic in Holland, the Herstedvester Institute in Denmark (founded by Georg K. Sturup), the Tavistock Institute in England, and by more than 240 institutions in the United States. California led the way.

T.M. Osborne (1859-1926) tried a few experiments in New York with prison self-management by the prisoners, but the experiments died with their author.

Ultra-Maximum Institutions

This brief history of penitentiaries would not be complete without a look at a relatively recent phenomenon: the ultra-maximum security prison.

A series of riots in the State of New York during the 1920s made authorities decide it was time to devise an institutions where such things could never happen. In 1931, Attica opened its doors. Security measures went to unheard-of extremes: heavily fortified towers, impenetrable walls, networks of electrically-controlled barriers, the rigid compartmentalization of the 2,000 inmates who were to be imprisoned there. Repression was the order of the day until 1971, when the worst prison riot ever to take place in the U.S.A. resulted in 43 dead and 300 wounded.

Another experiment in the ultra-maximum prison was the infamous Alcatraz.

The unprecedented economic crisis of the 1930s in the United States was accompanied by an unprecedented crime wave. The justice minister of the day, H.S. Cumming, accordingly called for the establishment of an ultra-maximum security prison for hardened offenders. Sanford Bates, the director of federal prisons, seconded the idea and won approval for it from President Roosevelt. If the United States could not feed her 25 million unemployed it would imprison them instead.

The site chosen for the new jail was an old fortress

dating from 1851, on an island near San Francisco, named Alcatraz. Workmen restored the existing buildings, reinforced their bars, and introduced observation towers, electrically-controlled barriers, observation posts and weapon-detecting systems. A constant maritime patrol of the surrounding coastline was maintained — quite unnecessarily, one would think, given the number of sharks already patrolling the area. The dream of sealing off the "hard-core" from the world had been realized.

This was to be the prison to end all prisons. Judges did not have to decide which prisoners to send there: this decision was left to the administrators of the other existing federal penitentiaries. Their choice fell on repeaters, hardened offenders, gangsters, — escape artists and trouble-makers. James A. Johnston, a former director of both San Quentin and Folsom, was put in charge of the new prison's administration. His approach was simple: repetition formed habits. As long as this basic truth was kept in mind, prisoners could be effectively controlled. Accordingly, the realistic, efficient answer was a programme of work which would far outstrip anything that had ever yet been tried.

The work programme consisted of a laundry, a clothing factory and a mattress factory. There was a series of strikes and, in 1946, a riot that finally had to be put down by the Marines, leaving five men dead in its wake. The prison was closed down in the early 1960s. It was no longer seen to be useful.

A final example in this category: the silent section of the Stuttgart-Stammheim prison, which opened in 1970 in the Federal Republic of Germany.

There are two interesting things about this chamber of horrors. The first is that the system is based on sensory deprivation — that is, the total or partial elimination of sensory stimuli (sounds, contrasts in light and shadow, and colours, all of which are essential to even the most elementary functioning). The second is that the first people affected by it, *outside Canada anyway*, were political militants accused of belonging to two extremist groups, the Red Army Fraction and the Socialist Collective of Heidelberg. The system called for total isolation, and total sensory deprivation.

"The régime of solitary confinement means: absolutely separate detention: the prisoner's isolation within the prison is reinforced by the installation over the bars on the windows of a fine netting or of metal strips which prevent any visual contact with the exterior; the prisoner must take his recreation period alone, so as to prevent his having any contact with other prisoners; they are forbidden participation in all normally collective activites, including showers and religious services; political censorship of books, papers, magazines and other printed matter, as well as exceedingly strict limitations on mail and visits;"[32]

Sensory deprivation is carried out in rooms which have been acoustically isolated from the external world, rooms painted completely white, with brilliant fluorescent lighting which remains on throughout the day so as to eliminate any shading in the room and thus deprive the prisoner of all sensory stimulation. This régime produces an inability to concentrate and to think coherently, or to orient oneself in space and time; it produces outbursts of rage and despair; visual, acoustical and tactile hallucinations; the sensation of splitting in two and of the loss of limbs; cardiac problems; hypersensitivity and hyperactivity when normal stimuli are restored.

Several of the prisoners who have been subjected to this system have suffered permanent mental and physical damage; some, like Holger Meins, committed suicide. Note, moreover, that this technique is used on people whose political and intellectual development renders them invulnerable to the more usual techniques, such as visits from psychologists and prison chaplains, designed to lead the prisoner to self-condemnation.[33]

Penitentiaries in Canada

Penitentiaries in Canada have evolved much as those in the rest of the world. There are some noteworthy particularities, however.

Legally, as pointed out in the Fauteux Report, "as early as 1843 the Legislature of the Province of Canada (which was a combination of the provinces of Upper Canada and Lower Canada) provided by legislation that a sentence of imprisonment of two years or more should be served in the provincial penitentiary at Kingston, while sentences of imprisonment for two years or less should be served in other penal institutions in the province.

"When the British North America Act was passed it gave to the Parliament of Canada legislative jurisdiction over penitentiaries and to the provinces legislative jurisdiction over other institutions. It made no provision as to the terms of imprisonment that should be served in one institution or the other.

"Parliament in 1869 provided that, by section 96 of chapter 29 of 32-33 Vict., 'each of the Penitentiaries in Canada shall be maintained as a Prison for the confinement and reformation of persons, male and female, lawfully convicted of crime before the Courts of Criminal Jurisdiction of that Province for which it is appointed to be the Penitentiary, and sentenced to confinement for life or for a term not less than two years; and whenever any offender is punishable by imprisonment, such imprisonment, if it be for life or for two years or any longer term, shall be in the Penitentiary.'

"This is, therefore, the basis for the distinction under Canadian law between sentences of two years or more, which are served in federal penitentiaries, and sentences of less than two years, which are served in provincial institutions. There is no basis in logic."

The first penitentiary in Canada was the one in Kingston, Ontario. It is worth noting what Sydney Shoom had to say about it in his article, *Kingston Penitentiary: The Early Decade*[34]. According to Shoom, in 1832 a resolution was passed in the House of Upper Canada which for the first time called for the construction of a penitentiary and voted the sum of £100 for the purpose. The first prisoners arrived in 1835, even though construction was not yet finished. This new prison also marked the first time authorities here co-operated with ones in the United States on penal matters, for the penitentiary was built under the supervision of a construction entrepreneur from Auburn and its first director was a former administrator with the clebrated Auburn prison. The Auburn system, therefore, was to have considerable influence on Kingston.

The régime at Kingston was harsh, especially in matters of corporal punishment. The standard punishment for any infraction of the rules of the prison was to be whipped with either the rawhide or the cat-o-nine-tails, the exact number of strokes depending on the offence. For example:

* Laughing and talking   6 lashes; cat-o-nine-tails
* Talking in wash-house   6 lashes; rawhide
* Threatening to knock   24 lashes; cat-o-nine-tails
  convict's brains out
* Staring about and inattentive   Bread and water
  at breakfast table
* Leaving work and going to   36 hours in dark cell, and
  privy when other convict   bread and water
  there

Despite the strict discipline, infractions were frequent. Shooms reports that in 1845, 2,102 punishments were meted out to 500 prisoners. Two years later, the number of punishments had risen to 6,063. During that period, each prisoner received corporal punishment an average of four or five times a year. Some mornings, twenty, thirty or as many as forty prisoners—men, women and children—received a public whipping. Certain cases are particularly shocking:

> * In 1841, Sarah O'Connor, aged 14, was whipped four times in the space of three months;
> * On Christmas Day, 1844, Alex Lafleur, aged 11, received 12 lashes for having spoken French;
> * In 1846, Peter Charbonneau, aged 10 and serving a 7-year sentence, was given the rawhide on 71 separate occasions for offences like "making faces" and "tricks at table."

In 1846, there were 16 children under 16 years of age in Kingston Penitentiary, and 75 adolescents between the ages of 16 and 20. Men and women worked together during the scheduled periods of forced labour, their work being to break rocks—to be used in the construction of a church! Details like these help us appreciate the edifying way in which this country was built.

A four-person inspection committee was established in 1859, undoubtedly as a result of the Brown Report of 1849 on the penitentiary. It was to present an annual report to the Secretary of State for Canada, for the attention of the Governor-General.

At the time of Confederation, 1867, the four inspectors for the four founding provinces (Ontario, Quebec, New Brunswick and Nova Scotia) became directors of penitentiaries for the whole of Canada.

Three institutions were then in existence, two of them — St. Jean and Halifax — joining Kingston to become the first three penitentiaries in the new country.

Severe overcrowding in Kingston caused authorities to recommend in 1870 that a new penitentiary be established, this one in Québec. An existing reformatory for young male delinquents was therefore converted, and some new cell blocks added. The complex was located in a suburb of Montréal, at St. Vincent de Paul.

By May 1873, work on the complex was more or less complete. A first transfer of 119 prisoners was therefore made from Kingston. They came by water, and were chained together for the duration of the trip. The honour of being the first prisoner in the new institution fell to a man named John Atkinson: he was 36 years of age, a day-labourer by occupation, and had been sentenced on April 6, 1872 to three years.

In 1875, the Penitentiaries Act replaced the directors committee with the new position of inspector of penitentiaries.

In 1880, the penitentiaries of St. Jean and Halifax were turned over to provincial authorities and a new and more adequate facility for long-term imprisonment, Dorchester, opened in New Brunswick.

Meanwhile, two new provinces entered Confederation and with them, two new institutions — Stoney Mountain, Manitoba (1875) and New Westminster, British Columbia (1878). In 1911, a penitentiary was built in Prince Albert, Saskatchewan, marking the first time brick was used as the primary construction material rather than stone.

The final institution in this first wave of construction was Collin's Bay, Ontario (not far from Kingston). These seven institutions — Kingston, St. Vincent de Paul, Dorchester, Stoney Mountain, New Westminster, Prince Albert and Collin's Bay — provided the infrastructure for more than a century of experiments in repression by the Canadian Penitentiary Service.

However, it was not entirely smooth sailing. Dreadful living conditions sparked numerous riots throughout the 19th century and the portion of the 20th century already under discussion.

In 1897, for example, the Minister of Justice ordered an investigation into mismanagement at St. Vincent de Paul. As a result, the director, Ouimet (brother of the Minister of Public Works, incidentally), was dismissed. There were intensive studies made throughout the period 1890-1925 into reorganization of the imprisonment system, although no major changes were in fact made.

Repeated denunciations in the daily press led to repeated administrative inquiries into charges of political interference. The pressure brought some modifications. Directors' meetings were reorganized. Visits were made to penitentiaries outside the country. There was a whole series of attempts made to find new ways to classify and segregate prisoners and to "humanize" the system. Urgent appeals were launched for better-trained, better-qualified personnel, and for better salaries with which to attract and keep them. Meanwhile, riots continued, thanks to the administrative delays and the general degradation found in all the institutions.

The economic crisis of 1911, however, put an end to reform. There was a new wave of riots in Kingston, St. Vincent de Paul and Dorchester, which was ruthlessly supressed. As Raymond Boyer said (in his paper cited above):

"Until 1913, prisoners had fire hoses turned on them; until 1933, they were constantly shackled; until 1938, they were being handcuffed to the bars of their cells for up to eight hours a day."[35]

As well, punishment by whip, strap and paddle was commonplace. These punishments were administered in the presence of prison employees and often in the presence of other prisoners. Such torture continued until very recently, as may be seen in the table in the Ouimet Report of officially-administered corporal punishments: ⟩

TABLE III
Use of Corporal Punishment in Canadian Penitentiaries as a Disciplinary Measure[36]

1957-15	1963-96 (St. Vincent de Paul riot)
1958-16	1964-26
1959-24	1965- 7
1960-12	1966-32
1961-67	1967-19
1962-18	1968- 1 (Jan.-Sept.)

Total: 333

The Archambault Report of 1938 had denounced this kind of treatment and made a long list of recommendations, none of which was taken up for several decades thereafter.

From 1946 to 1960, the Canadian Penitentiary Service was under the direction of a former military man, Major-General Ralph Gibson. During his tenure, the number of institutions rose from 7 to 15, some minor reforms were made and a very limited expansion of psychiatric services in the institutions took place. It was, however, toward the end of this military régime that the Correctional Planning Committee (1958-1959) was established, its purpose being to suggest the appropriate restructuring of the entire Canadian penitentiary system, including policy on parole. The committee report, submitted in 1959, was known as the MacLeod Report for its chairman, Allen Joseph MacLeod, Q.C. MacLeod was a lawyer who had gone to work for the Ministry of Justice in 1945 and was successively legal counsel for the ministry, director of its Criminal Law Section, director of the Remission Service (renamed the National Parole Service in 1959), and finally, in 1960, became the first outsider to be appointed Commissioner of Penitentiaries. The Canadian Penitentiary Service had its second wave of development during his administration.

MacLeod remained commissioner until 1970, when he became special counsellor to the Ministry of the Solicitor-General, a position he held until his retirement in 1974.

It was an error, obviously, to have the major reforms of the Sixties carried out by the man who had recommended them. As in many other political sectors, changes in the field of penitentiaries have much more to do with the socio-economic circumstances of the day than with the personality of a self-styled "enlightened" director.

By the end of MacLeod's tenure in 1970, not only had the number of institutions risen from 9 to 34, but it had become politically desirable to endow the country with an enlarged, improved, infrastructure for repression.

The Penitentiaries Act was revised in 1960, following the presentation of the MacLeod Report the previous year. One major change was that the prison warden lost exclusive responsibility for decisions about the detention of prisoners for security reasons. The traditional paternalistic system, whose passing was lamented by none, had been replaced by a strongly bureaucratic one.

In 1961, Justice Minister Fulton announced to the House of Commons the establishment of both a five-year and a ten-year construction programme, to be accompanied by radical changes in the way penitentiaries were run. The cabinet approved the plans without hesitation. Farewell to the Dark Ages; henceforth, light would penetrate even the smallest nooks and crannies of the system! The whole programme, of course, was to be widely publicized, with the media playing their accustomed role of persuading public opinion to endorse government politices. In future, it would not be a matter of punishing criminals, but of "treating delinquents."

Let us note, however, that corporal punishment was not abolished for another seven years. And there is still the very real possibility that this legal form of torture will be re-established.

When questioned on this subject during his appearance before the parliamentary Sub-Committee on the Penitentiary System in Canada, Commissioner André Therrien replied that he was not opposed to all forms of corporal punishment. Whatever his views, prison employees continue to grant themselves the right to harass prisoners.[37]

But it took more than the MacLeod Report and the decision of the Minister of Justice finally to bring about reforms which alleviated, at least in part, the conditions in which prisoners had to live.

What finally sparked some action on the ten-year plan was the famous St. Vincent de Paul uprising in 1962, the worst riot ever to occur in a Canadian penitentiary. It was caused by the frightful living conditions in an institution which had been condemned by the 1938 Archambault Commission. Yet one could justifiably conclude that, although the riot hastened the reforms, it had scarcely any impact on living conditions in St. Vincent de Paul itself, for in the period 1960-1975, 48 prisoners committed suicide behind its walls. Since that amounts to almost half of all prisoner suicides in Canada, that statistic led Solicitor-General MacIllrith to order a formal inquiry in 1970. It had already caused Justice Minister Guy Favreau to declare, during the 1960s, "What I'd like to do is plant a bomb under St. Vincent de Paul and blow that relic of the Middle Ages off the face of the earth."[38]

The history has yet to be written of the misery suffered by the 150,000 people who have passed through St. Vincent de Paul since it first opened its doors. One chapter of any such book would certainly have to be devoted to the brutal repression carried out by the Canadian Army and the Royal Canadian Mounted Police in the months following the 1962 riot.

And so, in 1963, the ten-year plan for the Canadian Penitentiary Service was set in motion. And revised in 1965. In brief, it called for new buildings and new administrative divisions, gave projections of expected future numbers of prisoners, and outlined general principles for their treatment. The emphasis was to be on control, rather than on security. "Control" may be defined as having the prisoners internalize the desired norms, through a variety of techniques, so that they effectively become their own jailers.

It was in the MacLeod era that we see for the first time the infamous distinction between maximum, medium and minimum-security institutions. It was also at this time that we first heard about the "Living Unit System"—for even the vocabulary was up-graded, so as to fit in with the reforms. Good-bye to "guards," "prisons" and "shit-disturbing"; hello to "correctional officers," "institutions" and "negative attitudes."

This new language was the semantic packaging for the two central elements of the new system: Living Units, and group therapy.

The Living Unit System was given conceptual shape under MacLeod, but not applied until 1971-72. It was explained to the parliamentary Sub-Committee in the following way:

> "The Living Unit System is basically a way of managing the day to day treatment of inmates in medium and maximum-security institutions. It differs from the conventional system in that the correctional officers concerned with internal security are replaced by Living Unit officers... The functions and responsibilities of the Living Unit officer are very different from those of the traditional correctional officer. The LU1 is not uniformed, but wears ordinary street dress. He has a case-load of between five and ten inmates with whom he works especially closely and in respect of whom he makes recommendations and reports concerning good conduct, temporary absences, parole, etc. His job combines many of the traditional functions of the classifications officer... One of the broad intentions behind deploying staff-members in this way is to improve both the control and the correctional effectiveness of the institution by improving the quality of the relationship between the staff-members and inmates."[39]

We touched on the subject of group therapy in the section on the general history of penitentiaries. During the MacLeod era, its use became widespread. Several experiments along such lines had been carried out in the Fifties, notably in St. Vincent de Paul in 1950, when members of the John Howard Society worked with some of the anglophone prisoners. Psychiatrists and psychologists remained unconvinced of the value of this therapy, however, and two criminologists, Fréchette and Ciale, tried the experiment again in 1956, this time with prisoners under 21 years of age. For its day, their methodology was quite revolutionary. They based their approach on psychoanalysis, and sought to establish favourable conditions for a relationship of transference to develop between the prisoners and themselves.

To do so, they concentrated on an exploration of problems and conflicts. They tried to convince the prisoner to abandon the defence mechanisms which he had built up as a way of protecting himself in the prison environment, and to drop his aggressive attitude toward society or the institution. The therapist's role (though this was never officially acknowledged) was to lead the prisoner to place maximum blame on himself for his situation. Experiments along this line continued to take place, often led by prison chaplains or volunteers, people with no special training for the position.

A more scientific experiment was carried out in 1971 at Ste. Anne des Plaines, with eight recidivists between the ages of 21 and 34. Specialists drew on Rogerian therapy, meditation techniques and film (to stimulate visual reactions) in their work.

But, as a generalized phenomenon, group therapy didn't make its appearance until the Sixties. That was the time when everything was being lumped under the banner of "healing." Another development was the opening of a few specialized institutions, such as Matsqui in British Columbia (1965) for the detention and treatment of drug addicts. Liberal measures like these, however, were accompanied by the opening in 1968 of the country's first *ultra*-maximum-security institution, the Special Detention Unit, of which we shall have more to say in a later chapter. Still, a certain liberalization did take place across the country: prisoners received apprenticeship training to a number of trades, the right to books, to correspondence, visits and to temporary absences. MacLeod also followed through on one of the major recommendations of the Fauteux Report, with the creation of the National Parole Service.

In 1959, the Governor-General in Council named five members to this new board, their task being to carry out the provisions of the law concerning parole. The board was expanded to nine in 1969, partly so as to permit an experiment in holding hearings right in the federal institutions themselves. Though their reports were often forwarded by the Solicitor-General to the government, the board, as a body, had considerably more decision-making power than any court.

As with any other agency of the federal government, the board had an established system of delegating authority to regional offices. As well, it worked closely with the various police forces of Canada, with judges' associations, etc...

Today, the board has 19 members, with backgrounds in such fields as criminology, psychology, social work, law, business, and prison and police administration. There are 700 employees, 300 of them parole officers. In 1976, the board made 16,000 decisions on parole, granted it in about 38% of cases, and supervised some 6,139 parolees (who each cost about $1,500 to maintain on parole, which is roughly one-tenth of what it takes to keep a person in prison).

The criteria used by the board appear to be rather vague, if one goes by the testimony of its chairman, W.R. Outerbridge, to the parliamentary Sub-Committee:

> "We want to try to mix the prejudices of various Board members and, hopefully, come up with a decision that will be more mature because it is more broadly based." However, as he had observed a moment earlier, "...But, essentially, when you come right down to it, what the alchemy is by which you come to the decision of yes or no is a subjective judgment, sure. It is a value judgment made by board members."[40]

Finally, it was during the MacLeod era, in 1965, that the Canadian Committee on Corrections was established. Its mandate is worth quoting, given the large number of studies published in the last decade on the subject of penitentiaries:

> "To study the broad field of corrections, in its widest sense, from the initial investigation of an offence through to the final discharge of a prisoner from imprisonment or parole, including such steps and measures as arrest, summonsing, bail, repre-

sentation in Court, conviction, probation, sentencing, training, medical and psychiatric attention, release, parole, pardon, post-release supervision and guidance and rehabilitation; to recommend as conclusions are reached, what changes, if any, should be made in the law and practice relating to these matters in order better to assure the protection of the individual and, where possible, his rehabilitation, having in mind always adequate protection for the community; and to consider and recommend upon any matters necessarily ancillary to the foregoing and such related matters as may later be referred to the Committee; but excluding consideration of specific offences except where such consideration bears directly upon any of the above mentioned matters."[41]

In short, governments have, over the years, reorganized the apparatus of repression so as to keep it well-adapted to the ever-expanding needs of the capitalist society which gives it life.

Paul Faguy was head of the Canadian Penitentiary Service from 1970 to 1974, the second outsider in its history to do so. The liberalization continued. Prisoners lost their numbers, for example (prisoners had been nameless, for central government purposes, since 1835), their uniforms began to look more like normal street clothes and they were allowed to have long hair and beards. Prisoner committees were encouraged (though the authorities did their best to co-opt them), and so were citizen committees. (Not entirely a new idea: a citizen committee had had the run of Kingston Penitentiary in 1835. But then, public support has always been a necessary element in any program of repression.) More and more evaluation officers were introduced into the system, good bureaucrats all. The Canadian Penitentiary Service received enormous increases in both budget and personnel.

Solicitors-General Goyer and Allmand each in turn led the major campaign for the replacement of the death penalty by sentences with no possibility of parole for the first 25 years. The campaign came to its climax in 1976, with the introduction of Bill C-84. But the era of liberalization was to end.

Despite the mass of qualifiers sprinkled through the text of the 1973 paper, *The Criminal in Canadian Society — A Perspective on Corrections*, which Solicitor-General Allmand prepared for a federal-provincial conference on corrections, it was clear that as the ten-year plan (1963-1973) drew to its close, authorities were preparing to take a harder line. As Prime Minister Trudeau told the House of Commons on May 16, 1973: "Our prisons are there to contain unlawful persons. Containment is the primary function. Rehabilitation follows."

A new task force was appointed in 1973. According to the testimony of Mr. A.T. Wabayashi, of the Ministry of the Solicitor-General, before the parliamentary Sub-Committee: "The Solicitor-General of Canada, in 1973, appointed a five-member task force with the responsibility of recommending ways and means of creating this new integrated federal corrections agency, which would include the National Parole Service and the Canadian Penitentiary Service."[42]

The Report of the Task Force on the Creation of an Integrated Canadian Corrections Service was submitted in 1977 under the title, *The Role of Federal Corrections in Canada*. Its orientation was made clear: the Sixties' ideal of reintegrating the offender into society came in for heavy criticism. One sub-head was the blunt, "Developing a Realistic Approach." Which translated into, "the offender is ultimately responsible for his criminal behaviour," and "the sentence of the court constitutes the punishment."[43]

The hard-line approach, which began under Faguy, grew more marked. (Temporary absences for prisoners fell from 65,000 in 1972 to 32,000 in 1973, the pretext being that prisoners took advantage of these leaves to commit more crimes.) Paroles fell off drastically as well, dropping from 4,368 in 1970 to 2,683 in 1973 and to 2,136 in 1976.

The logical consequence of the report by the Task Force on the Creation of an Integrated Canadian Corrections Service was the adoption of a bill authorizing indeterminate sentences and abolishing statutory pardons. As accompaniment, the new solicitor-general announced that 24 new penitentiaries were to be built, and that the parliamentary Sub-Committee was to be sent across the country, scouring the land for a solution...

How are we to explain this switch from a rather lengthy period of liberalization to one in which we shall be imprisoning more people, for longer periods of time, in appalling conditions?

The answer lies in the clever way in which the authorities have used the appearance of progressive steps (treatment for prisoners, humanization of sentences) to win public approval for an enormous machinery of repression (from 15 institutions to the more than 78 scheduled for completion by the end of 1980) and for a positively extravagant increase in the funds devoted to the purpose (from a budget of $16 million in 1959, to one of $308 million in 1977). As Allmand said in the introduction to his 1973 paper, *The Criminal in Canadian Society;* "We must win public approval for the necessary measures and expenditures..."[44]

Once the budgets are voted and the institutions built, the "treatment/repression" ambiguity, source of endless controversy, will no longer need to be so carefully maintained.

Canada will enter a new era. Fox has confirmed it: from now on the function of penitentiaries will be to protect society. And the prisoners function will simply be to behave themselves...

PART THREE:
The Political Role of the Penitentiary

Photo Credit: Cornell Capa. Attica.

CHAPTER 1
An Integrated Institution

This brief history of penitentiaries shows that the institution of the penitentiary has evolved, and that this evolution has not taken place in isolation. For example, the Catholic church, the dominant force for integration for several centuries, had a huge influence on the development of the incarceration system, and the countries of the Protestant Reformation, birthplace of the capitalist mode of production, brought to the treatment of prisoners the ideological elements of the new interrelationships of production, work and Bible study.

The limitations of this work obviously do not allow us to make an exhaustive list of the many ties weaving society and its penitentiaries together. But it is worth pointing out some of them.

The Gloucester model which came to the forefront in 18th-century England developed after the loss of the American colonies. Thereafter, the deportation of prisoners, which until then had been the common practice, was limited to Australia (until the 1860s). The metropolis therefore devised an approach to complement that of punishment, which was already in force, and gave this new role to the penitentiary. The French Revolution substituted loss of liberty for corporal punishment, but it would be a mistake to see this as a purely humanitarian act. The bourgeoisie, the new dominant class, was based on free enterprise: thus, the greatest possible punishment for the guilty party would be to be deprived of this "freedom," motor of the economic system. One must also understand that the new approach to repression was linked to a "new economic policy of the right to punish," to use Foucault's expression, which was to assure a greater social stability. The grills and bars of the penitentiary were to be more effective than the gallows in the public square. And one must recall that when the United States, in its turn, developed the modern penitentiary system in the post-revolutionary period of the late 18th and early 19th centuries, the country was racked by deep economic crisis and successive waves of popular unrest (which took the form of land occupations and tax revolts) that posed a serious threat to the new State. A system of incarceration, combined with armed repression, assured bourgeois control of the country as a whole. Always in the name of combatting criminality, of course.

The second wave of penitentiary construction in the United States, from 1850 to 1920, took place during the era of massive industrialization of the country and the emergence of America as the leader of the capitalist world.

Takagi has put together a telling chart of the systematic repression suffered by the working class during that period.

TABLE IV
Imprisonment in the United States
in the 19th century[45]

Year	Prison Population	Ratio of the Population as a Whole
1850	6,737 prisoners	1/3,442
1860	19,086 prisoners	1/1,647
1870	32,901 prisoners	1/1,171
1880	58,609 prisoners	1/855
1890	82,329 prisoners	1/757

And when one stops to examine the period when the penitentiaries came under attack (1890-1925), one is struck by how widespread that criticism was. The abuses of the capitalist system in the urban milieu, in factories, in short throughout society, set off a "reformist movement" that was to provide critical analyses of the system for the next three decades.

And so, the attacks on the penitentiaries were joined by bitter attacks on the packing houses of Chicago, the steel mills of Pittsburgh and the slums of Philadelphia and New York.

Penitentiaries, in the eyes of their detractors, were part and parcel of society's institutions as a whole. It is interesting to compare the turmoil going on in society during the terrible years of the Depression in the United States with the uprisings which were taking place in American prisons at the same time. Each phenomenon was met by the authorities in the same repressive way.

Take, for example, the joint strike of 1,000 hosiery and textile workers in North Carolina in 1929. It lasted two months and exacted a terrible toll: 7 dead, 24 wounded and about 150 strikers arrested [46]. That same year, mutinies in the Auburn and Clinton penitentiaries in the State of New York were also repressed by the armed forces: deaths and injuries were the result in those places as well.

The great penitentiary reforms of the 1960s, with their emphasis on the role of the intellectuals (psychologists, criminologists, etc.), are to be understood as the power structure's way of seeking to refine still further repression at every level. The reason for this effort lies in the fact that the extreme complexity of today's means of production (computers, massive automation, high technology) demand an ever-increasing degree of overall social control.

Psychologists have taken their place in medium-security penitentiaries; psychiatrists have taken *their* place in General Motors, to ensure that workers maintain the appropriate rhythm on the assembly line.

CHAPTER 2
Capitalism, Society and the State

The same approach which led us to analyze the legitimizing ideology for the penitentiary system, to examine the effects of incarceration (which are the exact opposite of the effects supposedly desired), to step back from prison experience to study the history of the institution and to trace its ties with the history of the larger societies in which it exists, now leads us to study the nature of the society which gave birth to the penitentiary system. Since we wish to define the preeminently political function of the penitentiary, this step is obviously of great importance.

We live in a capitalist society.

The statement is obvious to a minority, irrelevant and provocative to the majority, but we think it important to make this statement and then define the condition and, above all, make the connection between the society and the institution of the penitentiary. It's a risky step because the classic rebuttal is always, "Yes, but, there are prisons in Russia, too, you know..." We shall return to that point.

Let us begin by defining capitalism, and the capitalist mode of production. Then we shall explain why one variety or another of the penal institutions exists everywhere in the world.

The essential element in the analysis of any society is the analysis of the mode of production of that society... in other words, the method of obtaining the means of existence, the material goods necessary for the satisfaction of social needs and individual survival.

If, for example, we know how our society produces its bread, its furniture, homes and clothing, we have taken an important step toward understanding what kind of society we live in. This demonstration may be somewhat theoretical but it is worth the effort, for it will lead us to an incomplete but true understanding of the framework of our existence. Back to the mode of production.

It has two constituent elements.

First, *the forces of production.* By that we mean the ensemble of the means of labour, methods of production, at the level of science and technology.

The automobile assembly plant provides us with a very good example. The electricity that powers the machines, the construction of the many components that go to make up the machines (ball-bearings, cogs), the quality-control procedures used to test the final product, the research and development division always trying to increase productivity... in other words, the number of automobiles produced per day... all these things, together, add up to the forces of production.

The second element of the mode of production is *the relationships of production.* That means, who owns the means of production.

If the auto assembly plant described above belongs to General Motors, which in turn belongs to a few large stock-holders, then it follows that the workers in the plant are not the owners. The workers in that plant sell their labour (skill, knowledge, physical endurance) for a salary.

We may therefore make a general distinction between two major social classes in our society. The one group, those who own the factories, companies, mines, transportation systems, etc., may be called the possessing class, or the bourgeoisie.

91

Those who work in the factories and companies or who have worked there (like the unemployed and those on welfare or those injured in industrial accidents, and prisoners as a whole) receive a salary, and are called the working class.

It is easy to see that the relationship between these two major social classes is unequal, since the salary paid the worker represents only part of the work which takes place. The profit goes to swell the capital of the owner. When we speak of the capitalist system, we mean a system in which all the instruments of production for things which are essential to everybody's survival are in the hands of a minority, a bourgeoisie, and in which the mass, the working class, works for this bourgeoisie in exchange for a salary. In a capitalist system, the mass of the people is thus exploited by a minority.

The fundamental law of such a system is to exploit workers as much as possible so that capital may increase as much as possible.

This kind of domination by the few of the many is possible because the dominant class (bourgeoisie) has equipped itself with the means of ensuring that workers stay in their place. The instruments of this domination are the police, the judges, and the prisons. Basically, they exist so that the bourgeoisie may continue to control the mass of the workers, and may continue to exploit them.

The bourgeoisie possesses an organism which sees to it that workers continue to obey, continue to arrive at the factory on time, continue to accept a miserable salary, continue to obey the law. This organism is the State.

And so we see that a capitalist society — like the one in which we live, since workers here do not own the means of production — is not simply a society in which both rich and poor people are to be found.

A capitalist society is one in which the poor must continue to work to enable the rich to grow even richer.

Now that we have the necessary theoretical understanding of the nature of capitalism, we may examine the role of the State in this kind of society.

There is a pluralist-democratic theory of the State, which argues, in the words of the English political scientist

Ralph Miliband:

> "...the state, subjected as it is to a multitude of conflicting pressures from organized groups and interests, cannot show any marked bias towards some and against others."

And so, according to this author, the role of the State is apparently "to accommodate and reconcile them all."[47]

In other words, the role of the State is that of neutral arbiter, designed to guarantee the checks and balances of power, so that no one interest may have undue influence on the organism and thus on the citizenry as a whole.

Obviously, it is sometimes difficult, when listening to a speech by the prime minister, to realize that the government which directs the State is not doing so in an unbiased fashion.

Take, for example, the anti-inflation bill passed in October 1975. Pierre Elliott Trudeau explained to the population that prices were rising in such dizzying fashion that it was absolutely necessary for the State to intervene, regulate both unions and company owners, and restrain both wages and prices — all for the common good. Bill C-73, in principle, was to affect both worker and boss, and put an end to inflation.

The State therefore took a position — of Olympian detachment, at least that is the way things were presented to us.

And what was the result?

Two years after it was passed, the controversial Bill C-73 had caused a reduction of about $14 million in company profits... and a reduction of $800 million in workers' pay-raises. What raises *were* gained had to be fought for tooth and claw.

This simple example (and any number of other examples of State intervention could be given, each with the same results) shows that the State in our society exists purely and simply to guarantee that companies may continue to exploit the working class.

This reality is not limited to Canada, and it is not limited to the age in which we live.

When the bourgeoisie overthrew virtually all the monarchies in the world and took political control, it arranged things so that the State was at its service, but draped in a show of neutrality called "democracy."

One may argue that in western countries free elections exist, and that the mass of the population is free to bring to power whatever party it chooses.

Right. But when we take a look at most political parties, their composition (primarily lawyers and businessmen), and their underlying economic interests, we see that this whole lovely facade is controlled by the most powerful economic group in the society: the bourgeoisie. Or, to put it another way, the nominal source of power is electoral, but its true source is financial.

We lack statistics in Canada to evaluate the economic power of the ownership minority, but this kind of study has been done in other countries and one can assume that things here are much the same.

Miliband reports that:

> "the most obvious form of [inequality in the ownership of property] is provided by England, where 1 per cent of the population owned 42 per cent of personal wealth in 1960, 5 per cent owned 75 per cent and 10 per cent owned 83 per cent."[48]

And he describes a similar situation south of the border:

> "As for the United States... in 1953... 1 per cent of the adults owned 76 per cent of corporate stock."[49]

Now let us return to the situation of prisoners in Canadian penitentiaries, confronted by the State.

Of course, whenever problems arise, we can hardly expect the Minister of Justice or the Solicitor-General to state that if prisoners are beaten in these Crown institutions, if other prisoners commit suicide, if basic rights are systematically violated, it is nonetheless all in a good cause because the role of the State is to crush workers so that companies may continue to pile up the profits.

Faced with such injustices, which are hard to conceal, the representatives of the State, prudently cloaked in their protective shield of neutrality (so that the mass of workers never realizes the objective role of the organism), solemnly

94

declare that the cause of the problem must be determined. The preferred band-aid solution is to order an inquiry.

And in troop the régime's firemen — minus hoses, water, and any other fire-fighting equipment.

The Inger Hansen inquiry studied the disgraceful use of gas at Millhaven and recommended that the wardens be given training courses in its use. The Vantour inquiry roundly denounced the penitentiary practice of isolation, but this form of punishment continues unabated in every institution. And so on...

And whenever a so-called "in-depth" study takes place, matters are carefully arranged so that those supposedly responsible for the problems are hauled up on the carpet (wardens, programmes, reforms, out-moded institutions), but the State itself and the political reasons for penitentiaries are left untouched. Indeed, it is a characteristic of capitalist societies to present all political problems as mere administrative difficulties.

To listen to the committees of inquiry, the situation is so confused in the penitentiaries (which, let us note in passing, are the most thoroughly researched of all State institutions, since not even a pencil may be purchased without due investigation at either the local or national level) that one may well ask (!) whether the warden is in control, or perhaps the head of the prisoners' committee.

A good example of this attitude is to be found in the endless string of questions put by one of the members of the MacGuigan Committee, Simma Holt — a specialist in the art of sowing confusion and disguising the true role of the State:

> "Who is the authority? Do you know who the boss of this institution is?" (in New Westminster).[50]
>
> "You have been telling me that you are in control of your institution and we find that you have no control. I have heard that you are in control and you really have no control..." (in Millhaven).[51]

Bear in mind that this Liberal MP, as she told Allan MacLeod, had been visiting prisons for 20 years[52]. With powers of perception like these, the good soul must have trouble telling the House of Commons doorman from the prime minister...

For any person possessed of a certain degree of social awareness (and who, obviously, is not a civil servant), deciphering a political institution, be it a penitentiary or any other, is a straightforward affair. Whatever may be the administrative, financial and organizational particularities, the analysis of power requires that one follow the pyramidal structure of scientific analysis. Thus, the holders of power within the Canadian Penitentiary System may be enumerated, starting from the top:

The financial backers of the party in power, the party which forms the government, the cabinet, the solicitor-general of Canada, the commissioner of penitentiaries and his principal advisors, the regional directors, the directors of the institutions and their administrations and, at the bottom, the employees, including the guards.

It is obviously in the interest of the true decision-makers to cause it to appear that the battles take place at intermediate and even lower levels in the hierarchy. As long as disputes pit regional director against the head of the prison guards' union, prisoners against the persons who watch over them, director against one of the solicitor's deputies, then the conflicts never take on a political dimension. They remain, instead, administrative difficulties. The State then periodically examines such apparent "root problems" as excessive bureaucratization or the delegation of discretionary power (for example, the years of prison-guard brutality at Millhaven), and sacrifices a few scapegoats (fires a few guards, etc.) as a token adjustment to the system.

Recommendation 20 of the MacGuigan report clearly affirms this hierarchical chain of command:

> "The penitentiary system must be clearly defined by a vertical management system with short lines of authority and communication between the top and bottom..."

If we look again at the classic Miliband formula, and refuse to allow ourselves to be fooled by the ideological flim-flam of the power structure, we can see that the role of the

State is structured to meet certain very precise requirements:

> "In capitalist society the state was above all the coercive instrument of a ruling class, itself defined in terms of its ownership and control of the means of production."[53]

The penitentiary system, along with the police, the courts and the army, are key elements in the web of coercion. The role of the penitentiary is to provide a means by which the established order may maintain physical and psychological control, and/or the threat of such control, over the millions of Canadian workers.

Now, to deal with the objection mentioned earlier, namely, that imprisonment is hardly the exclusive weapon of the capitalist system since so-called "socialist" countries have retained this same form of oppression. A few comments are in order, which will help clarify, though not exhaust, the issue.

For one thing, even though revolutions have wrought major political changes in those countries, the capitalist mode of production has survived. This means, first, that the work done by workers in those countries is remunerated. Surplus value still exists, only the State replaces the Capitalist class, and appropriates it. The State, in socializing the means of production, replaced the former bourgeois class which had controlled the means of production with the State itself, and a new controlling class (which we may call the "State bourgeoisie") now controls the levers of power.

Capitalism has survived in those countries because the Party concentrated exclusively on a political revolution. Though "free-enterprise" capitalism has been replaced by State capitalism, the same inexorable laws of the exploitation of the worker and the accumulation of capital still apply.

As a result, the State — no longer industry's buttress but rather itself the embodiment of all its functions, including the maintenance of a system of repression and thus of a variety of forms of imprisonment — is itself maintained.

One may therefore state that to the degree that, and as long as, revolutionary movements fail to abolish the State outright and all its component elements, penitentiaries will survive.

This said, let us now examine the role of the State and of penitentiaries within monopoly capitalism—which is the stage we have reached in Canada today.

CHAPTER 3
The Apparatus of Repression in Monopoly Capitalism

We have briefly explored the characteristics of the capitalist system, of the State and of penitentiaries... We shall now seek to explain the way in which the Canadian Penitentiary System makes it possible for monopoly capitalism in this country to survive and to increase its power.

First, a few comments on those "monopolies" and the basic notions of "surplus" and of "absorption of surplus" within such a system.

Capitalism, like any other economic system, undergoes changes and mutations, but these changes, obviously, do not affect its fundamentals — the accumulation of capital thanks to the exploitation of workers and the firm support of the State. After 1890, capitalism began changing from a competitive system to a monopolistic one. In other words, we have moved from a market in which a very large number of companies fought bitter price wars, to a society in which extremely large firms, through the double process of absorbing other companies and of combining bank and industrial capital, have created financial capital. The effects of this mutation on the market are enormous. According to Baran and Sweezy:

> "One may briefly explain it by saying that in a competitive system, the individual company is a 'price taker' while in a monopoly-capitalism system, the big corporation is a 'price maker'."[54]

Naturally, the economic goals are unchanged:

> "The major goals of modern large-scale business are high managerial incomes, good profits, a strong competitive position, and growth."[55]

The result being, of course, even more revenue for the company.

> "The whole motivation of cost reduction is to increase profits and the monopolistic structure of markets enables the corporations to appropriate the lion's share of the fruits of increasing productivity in the form of higher profits."[56]

Which leads us to the notion of surplus:

> "...under monopoly capitalism, declining costs imply continuously widening profit margins. And continuously widening profit margins in turn imply aggregate profits which rise not only absolutely but as a share of national profit. If we provisionally equate profits with society's economic surplus, we can formulate a law of monopoly capitalism that the surplus tends to rise both absolutely and relatively as the system develops."[57]

The most succinct possible definition of this "economic surplus" is provided by the same authors:

> "the difference between what society produces and the costs of producing it."[58]

The departments of statistics of various governments, charged with the responsibility of keeping track of administrative data, have not so far included in their preoccupations any of the data relating to economic surplus.

This surplus, of course, constitutes an important percentage of the Gross National Product (GNP) of a country, the GNP being everywhere defined as "the market value of all the finished products and services for a year," the equivalent of the national revenue plus net indirect taxes (indirect taxes minus subsidies) plus deductions for depreciation and other such business expenses.

For the purposes of our analysis, it is important to note that economic surplus grows along with the GNP.

Here is the growth of the GNP in Canada for the last thirty years.

TABLE V
Gross national product of Canada[59]
(in billions, real dollars)

1946-11.885	1957-33.513	1968- 72.586
1947-13.169	1958-34.777	1969- 79.815
1948-15.127	1959-36.846	1970- 85.685
1949-16.800	1960-38.359	1971- 93.462
1950-18.491	1961-39.646	1972-103.952
1951-21.640	1962-42.927	1973-120.438
1952-24.588	1963-45.978	1974-144.616
1953-25.833	1964-50.280	1975-161.132
1954-25.918	1965-55.364	1976-184.494
1955-28.528	1966-61.828	
1956-32.058	1967-66.409	

With an average annual growth of 9.65% since 1945, there is reason to state that the giant corporations have managed to achieve a considerable increase in production. But it would be a mistake to assume that all society has benefited. Quite the reverse.

Although a few groups of workers, the best-organized ones, have managed in highly industrialized countries like Canada to gather a few more crumbs from the table, we must not forget that they have done so at the expense of the majority of workers, both here in Canada and in the rest of the world. Two-thirds of the population of the "under-developed" part of the world are, literally, hungry. This shameful situation is obviously the result of world-wide exploitation. Almost no research has been done in Canada to determine what percentage of our total GNP is represented by economic surplus.

Let us therefore give ourselves a rough estimate of such a figure by noting what statistician Joseph D. Phillips had to say about the GNP of the United States and economic surplus:

> "...the magnitude of the surplus in the United States amounted to 46.9 per cent of Gross National Product in 1929... reaching 56.1 per cent in 1963."[60]

Once again, the important thing to remember is the following: the Canadian GNP has risen at an average annual rate of 9.65% for the last thirty years, and at 11.61% for the last ten years. Therefore, the economic surplus is following the same curve.

(Tedious as this material may seem, it is of great importance for our eventual understanding of the extraordinary expansion of the penitentiary system in Canada. The sums of money devoted to that system at first seem absurd, but they have real economic logic behind them.)

Monopolies, in their pursuit of the accumulation of capital, are faced with two major problems: one is to accumulate ever more profit; the other is to absorb the economic surpluses in order to create even more profits.

The first of these problems looks for its solution in technological innovation, new management methods and the armed pillage of the resources of the "under-developed" countries. The greater challenge is posed by the second problem, that of absorbing the surplus.

Investments are one means, but others are needed as well. This is why we have seen the enormous growth of parasite sectors such as advertising, which swallows massive sums of money ($20 billion in the United States in 1963, as compared to $3.4 billion in 1929) as it churns out campaigns designed to increase demand... and thus profits. The social value of this activity, of course, is nil.

But it is the State which does the most to solve the problem of how to absorb economic surplus.

We have noted that in western countries the State has always seen to it that corporations' profits increase, whether by providing direct subsidies or by reducing the costs of production (e.g., Bill C-73).

In the monopolist stage of capitalism, the State also plays a key role in the absorption of surplus. Baran and Sweezy explain it very well:

> "Strengthening monopoly and regularizing its operations are of course not the only functions of the state under monopoly capitalism... The state, through its taxing and spending activities and through its policies toward the rest of the world, plays a decisive role in the way the system operates."[61]

In a country like the United States, post-World War Two military expenditure alone has clearly played a crucial role in the absorption of surplus.

In Canada, various sectors, including the one of repression (and thus the Canadian Penitentiary Service), carry out the same economic mission.

Let us look at the sums devoted to the penitentiaries since 1947.

TABLE VI
Cost of the penitentiary system in Canada[62]
(real dollars)

1947- 3,654,072	1958-12,215,295	1969- 60,822,000
1948- 4,247,884	1959-16,189,462	1970- 69,980,513
1949- 4,708,658	1960-19,149,395	1971- 75,096,619
1950- 5,270,860	1961-18,362,862	1972- 79,843,319
1951- 6,121,254	1962-22,299,000	1973- 86,357,155
1952- 6,955,970	1963-24,126,000	1974-115,000,000
1953- 7,364,148	1964-26,045,000	1975-138,798,549
1954- 8,860,419	1965-37,434,193	1976-256,000,000
1955-10,137,785	1966-54,600,000	1977-308,600,000
1956-10,331,759	1967-57,304,867	
1957-11,607,390	1968-63,200,000	

We have now established that the average annual rate of increase for the last thirty years has been 16.93%, and for the last ten years 19.72% — a similar phenomenon to that noticed earlier concerning governmental expenditures and the rise of the GNP. We may now properly clarify the close relationship between these two indices.

But we must first examine the system's traditional excuses for the amount of money being spent on the prisons.

104

CHAPTER 4
The System's Objections

Let us take a moment to consider the counter-arguments to our thesis.

Several objections may be raised to this kind of interpretation of the economic utility of the prison system to the business world.

For example, it may be said that the vast majority of the 10,000 or so prisoners produce nothing and that the money spent on them is therefore pure waste.

It is true that most prisoners twiddle their thumbs and that those who do work still don't add much to the year-end GNP.

The Canadian Penitentiary Service has released some figures on this subject. In 1949, the total production by the penitentiaries' 4,225 inmates amounted to $1,434,775.11. "Production" covers not only manufacturing (mail bags, for example), but farm work and prison maintenance as well. Fourteen years later, with a growth of about 70% in the prisoner population, total production had risen to $1,618,403 — a rise of 12 per cent.

But one must not forget that the purpose of imprisonment in the monopoly capital stage is not the same as it was during the stage of the primitive accumulation of capital. During the 19th century, prisoners were sentenced to hard labour. And in the work camps of the "socialist" countries, the prisoners are put to a whole variety of tasks. The Moscow subway system and a number of hydro-electric dams in the USSR were built in this way. China seems to follow the same principle. "Rehabilitation through work," as they say. But in fact, it amounts to making use of cheap labour.

It is not well known that in 1859 there was a movement afoot in Canada to make the territory of Hudson's Bay into a penal colony. The idea was reborn in 1887: the American Penal Congress, meeting in Toronto, discussed the possibilities of setting up a penal colony in northern Canada and Alaska. The proposal surfaced once again during the great economic crisis of 1929. In 1930, the Bennett government set up a concentration camp for the stubborn Doukhobor minority (Russian immigrants at the end of the 19th century who had resisted the Czarist régime and had been financed in their wanderings by the writer Leo Tolstoy) on Peers Island between Vancouver and Victoria. The camp lasted until 1935.

There were also, from 1933 to 1936, forced labour camps for the unemployed. Some 40,000 workers, primarily in western Canada but also in the Mont-Tremblant region and in the Valcartier camp, built roads and military barracks for the grand salary of 20 cents a day!

In Canada, as in other countries, prison production is insignificant. One must not be mislead into thinking, however, that the economic function of the institution is also insignificant.

In the first place, penitentiaries absorb some of the economic surplus. (Here we may usefully compare the respective percentage growth of the GNP and the penitentiary budget.)

In the second place, imprisonment assures social stability which in turn allows Canadian corporations to increase their profits in dramatic fashion.

As we said in our brief historical review, the penitentiary is a profitable exercise for the powers that be: the imprisonment of a very small number of people causes the very great majority to work within the system and accept its values.

This is clearly demonstrated by a comparison of prisoners to the population as a whole:

TABLE VII
By decade, the number of prisoners in proportion to
Total population[63]

Year	Population of Canada	Number of Prisoners	Ratio
1881	4,324,810	1,218	1/3,550
1891	4,833,239	1,258	1/3,869
1901	5,371,315	1,382	1/3,886
1911	7,206,643	1,865	1/3,912
1921	8,787,949	2,150	1/4,087
1931	10,376,786	3,714	1/2,783
1941	11,506,655	4,688	1/3,120
1951	14,009,429	4,817	1/3,438
1961	18,238,000	6,637	1/3,639
1971	21,600,000	7,458	1/3,452

We see that the present ratio of prisoners to general population is about the same as it was in 1881. This means that, despite the expansion of the apparatus of repression, power in Canada is still relatively easy to exercise.

If we look at this phenomenon in its larger context, we see that the imprisonment of some 20,000 people (prisons plus penitentiaries) permits the effective control of 22 million. In the United States, multiple pressures upon the system require that this proportion be doubled—out of a total population of some 215,000,000, about 500,000 are in detention in the various penal institutions. But even with one citizen out of 450 imprisoned in the United States (compared to one out of 1,100 in Canada), social control, though widespread and repressive, remains largely economical.

Another argument used against our thesis about the role played by penitentiaries in the absorption of surplus is the one often invoked by the power structure itself, namely: "If costs are increasing, it is because criminal behaviour is increasing, therefore we must imprison more people." Or: "The number of people being imprisoned is rising." Or: "It is more and more expensive to keep people in prison."

Let's look at this argument, "Crime is increasing."

We'll start with the following table which shows the number of people found guilty of criminal acts in Canada between 1949 and 1968, and thus liable to a prison sentence.

This seems to us a more concrete way to proceed than to examine the number of infractions committed each year, for the simple reason that penitentiaries hold only those who have been found guilty, not all those who have committed offences.

It would obviously have been useful to be able to give the figures for the last nine years, but the type of statistics which have been published separate Alberta and Québec from the rest of Canada, and it seems impossible to reconcile the two sets of data. Even so, the picture we can give is a significant one.

TABLE VIII
Number of people found guilty
of criminal acts[64]

1949-30,922	1956-27,413	1963-42,914
1950-31,434	1957-31,765	1964-42,097
1951-28,980	1958-34,546	1965-41,832
1952-29,761	1959-31,092	1966-45,670
1953-29,567	1960-35,443	1967-45,703
1954-30,848	1961-38,679	1968-49,963
1955-28,273	1962-38,663	

With an average annual increase of 2.94% in the number of people found guilty of criminal acts, the political authorities have absolutely no justification for the way they are overloading the nation's penitentiaries. Especially given that (for example) at the end of 1976 a full 44.3% of the prisoners were there for non-violent crimes.[65]

The average length of sentence handed down by the courts is 7.3 years.[66]

This is another way of saying that the number of people being convicted in Canada is not rising, taking into account the increase in population as a whole; rather, *the authorities are being more and more repressive with those who are convicted.* As we have already said, in 1927—a generally harsh era untouched by any notion of "humanization"—2,000 of the 2,480 prisoners in federal penitentiaries were serving sentences of 2 to 8 years.[67] We have "progressed" since then: what used to be the maximum penalty for most has now become the average sentence length for all.

Bruno Cormier was right when he said, in 1970: "The law of preventive detention in Canada is the most severe one imaginable."[68]

This objection, of course, is always buttressed with the preferred argument of demagogues of every stripe, the one about the "horrifying" rise in violent crime. Once again, the statistics compiled by Statistics Canada contradict the sweeping generalizations. Look at the following table:

TABLE IX
Violent crimes* and their percentage relationship to other offences under the criminal code, Canada 1966-1973

Year	Offences under the Criminal Code	No. of Violent Crimes	% of Violent Crimes in Comparison with Other Crimes under the Criminal Code
1966	702,809	69,656	9.9
1967	786,071	77,614	9.9
1968	897,530	87,544	9.8
1969	994,790	95,084	9.6
1970	1,109,988	102,358	9.2
1971	1,166,457	108,095	9.3
1972	1,189,805	110,468	9.3
1973	1,298,551	114,760	8.8

The evidence, therefore, shows that although the absolute number of violent crimes is rising, as a *percentage* of all crimes it is tending to drop. And, moreover, that violent crime has never been even 10% of all crime.

If we now seek the reason for crime itself, we must acknowledge the words of Manual Lopez-Rey y Assoyo in a report to the United Nations:

> "Since it is inherent to every society, criminality as such cannot be eliminated. It may, however, be considerably reduced by the development of a type of national or international society in which the evil effects of conditioning factors (inequality, penal systems, power) are reduced to a reasonable minimum."[69]

---

* Violent Crimes: Murder, attempted murder, assault, rape, involuntary homicide, aggravated theft, sexual offences, assault and battery.

And so we see that the "rising crime" argument explains nothing about the maintenance and expansion of the penitentiary system. Now let us look at the "overcrowding in the prisons" argument.

When questioned on this subject, the authorities invariably reply that the number of prisoners is increasing by some 4% to 5% a year. The claim, as any examination reveals, is highly exaggerated.

In the words of ex-commissioner MacLeod, during his testimony to the sub-committee:

> "We predicted in the early nineteen-sixties... that there was an imbalance in annual increase in penitentiary population of about 4 per cent. We found in our experience that some years it went down to 1 per cent but then within three years it was up to 8 or 9 per cent, and it did average out at 4 per cent."[70]

Michel Le Corre, Québec regional director, went further, in his testimony to the sub-committee. He estimated the annual increase to be in the vicinity of 18% to 20% per year.

The next table shows the increase in the number of penitentiary inmates since 1930:

TABLE X
The number of inmates in the penitentiaries
(1930-1977)[71]

1930-3,187	1946-3,362	1962-7,156
1931-3,714	1947-3,752	1963-7,219
1932-4,164	1948-3,851	1964-7,651
1933-4,587	1949-4,225	1965-7,514
1934-4,220	1950-4,750	1966-7,437
1935-3,552	1951-4,817	1967-7,185
1936-3,098	1952-4,686	1968-7,027
1937-3,264	1953-4,934	1969-7,160
1938-3,580	1954-5,120	1970-7,375
1939-3,803	1955-5,507	1971-7,458
1940-3,772	1956-5,508	1972-7,779
1941-3,688	1957-5,433	1973-8,827
1942-3,232	1958-5,770	1974-8,610
1943-2,968	1959-6,295	1975-8,580
1944-3,078	1960-6,344	1976-8,994
1945-3,129	1961-6,637	1977-9,338

Calculations reveal that the average percentage increase per year in the number of prisoners in the institutions has in fact been 2.38 per cent—about half the figure claimed by the ex-commissioner. Since nobody ever double-checks this kind of statistic, the power structure is able to frighten the population, and get its budgets accepted.

But one more thing must be said about this pseudo-overpopulation: it is a red herring. It is a red herring for the simple reason that the power structure has complete control over the penitentiary—that is, the number of people sentenced to the institutions—and the rate of exit from the penitentiary, that is, the number of people granted parole.

Since the judges (nominated by the political party in power) are growing more and more severe (we must make an example, you know), and since the Parole Commission is ever more careful about granting parole (only 38% of parole requests are granted, and the requests come from only a small fraction of the 9,300 inmates), there is every reason to conclude that if there is "overcrowding" in the penitentiaries, it is because the State wants it.

Moreover, with the explosion of twenty-five-year sentences (700 prisoners in Canada have been sentenced to this madness), with Bill C-51 planning to abolish statutory reductions and impose indefinite sentences, and with Francis Fox spreading the word that he needs 24 new penitentiaries (including a few in his own riding) in the next few years, one may well assume that the number of prisoners is going to rise. For penitentiaries are just like expressways: they are built to eliminate bottlenecks and then, a few years later, we find that the number of vehicles has doubled...

The claim of overpopulation, as we have seen, is perhaps the weakest of the justifications being used by the Canadian Penitentiary Service. Especially since its own commissioner, M. Therrien, sometimes makes statements that flatly contradict the argument:

> "If I had assurances that the courts of the country would stop sending people to me, or that they would send only half of those they do at this time in the next 2 or 3 years, maybe we would not need that construction programme. We are not providing now for an augmentation of the inmate population, we are just trying to replace some of these old places."[72]

Finally, let us consider the argument that "it is increasingly expensive to keep the inmates," and, therefore, the penitentiary system itself becomes more expensive.

Here again, we thought it useful to study the facts.

What we are attacking here is the hoary myth, "the prisoner lives in the lap of luxury"... "every inmate costs the community $15,000 a year," etc...

We looked at the period 1947-1968 and studied the breakdown of expenses. Note that sometimes certain costs do not appear in the totals, and vice versa.

TABLE XI
Staff salaries, and maintenance of prisoners[73]

Year	Staff Salaries	Prisoner Maintenance
1947	$ 2,605,591	$ 641,936
1948	2,313,701	766,087
1949	2,756,104	976,899
1950	3,023,238	1,146,170
1951	3,520,459	1,330,009
1952	4,052,178	1,469,361
1953	4,430,683	1,489,283
1954	4,759,955	1,546,610
1955	5,201,863	1,590,702
1956	5,693,155	1,790,415
1957	—	—
1958	7,512,818	1,798,730
1959	7,949,688	2,057,920
1960	8,687,453	2,337,274
1961	10,388,222	2,453,492
1962	11,634,749	3,058,367
1963	13,105,818	3,574,426
1964	13,750,218	3,758,130
1965	16,216,827	3,957,361
1966	18,170,703	4,337,684
1967	27,503,793	4,737,418
1968	29,309,000	—

N.B.: the missing figures could not be located.

As we see, the amount of money devoted to the maintenance of prisoners keeps dropping in relationship to the salaries being paid staff. In 1947, the amount allocated to prisoners was 24.6% of that allocated to staff salaries. In 1967, the number of prisoners had nearly doubled (from 3,752 to 7,185), but the proportion of the budget allocated to them had dropped to 17.2 per cent.

There has been a phenomenal increase in the last decade in the number of employees in the Canadian Penitentiary Service. In 1967, there were 4,262 employees; in 1977, about 9,168. In other words, the number has doubled. The employee: prisoner ratio has dropped from 1:1.68 to 1:1, and we may very confidently argue that the amount of money spent on prisoners no longer represents any more than about 10% of the amount being paid the personnel in salaries.

When you add in the fact that life for a great many prisoners, especially those in maximum-security institutions (in 1976, 40.4%), consists of spending 23 hours a day in their cells and that their meals are estimated to cost about 50 cents each, then you may conclude that the part of the budget devoted to the prisoners of the Canadian Penitentiary Service is becoming even smaller. Yet, despite all this, the authorities go on claiming that each convict costs the community $15,000 a year!

In fact, the lion's share of the cost of prisoner maintenance goes to the meals. In 1974-75, this was estimated at 52 cents per meal, for 8,580 inmates and 11 million meals — in other words, an expense of $5,720,000 out of a total budget of nearly $139 million!

In the past fifty years, the Canadian Penitentiary Service has gone from 6 to 55 institutions, and a staff: prisoner ratio of 1:5 to 1:1. One may therefore conclude that the increase in prison expenditures has had very little to do with improving conditions for the prisoner, and a great deal to do with the hiring of additional personnel, pay raises for that personnel, and the construction of new institutions. The authorities may reply that improving the structures increases the possibilities of rehabilitation. Nothing could be further from the truth.

In 1950, 77.13% of prisoners had a previous record. In 1977, the percentage was about the same. What is costing the community more and more is not the maintenance of prisoners, since that amounts to three meals a day (of very dubious quality), but rather, the maintenance of an enormous system of repression.

Now for the final bogeyman in this assortment of

justifications for the penitentiary system: it exists to protect the lives of the citizens. Let us select two years in the past decade and compare two phenomena in those years which resulted in the death of citizens and governmental action in each instance.

In 1970, 430 people were murdered in Canada. In that same year, 4,483 people died in fatal automobile accidents. That is, there were 10.42 times as many deaths arising from the policies regulating our transportation system as there were from the actions of murderers. (And note: about 70% of the murders were committed by people who already knew their victims—family, neighbours, work-mates...) In 1973, three years later, 474 people were murdered and 6,522 died in auto accidents. That is, we had a 10.23% increase in the first category, and a 45.48% increase in the second.

And what has the State done about it?

Since political hay may be made of murders (as a justification for increased repression), the number of policemen was increased in this period from 48,548 to 56,117—with all the gains in social control that we have already mentioned, though no noticeable impact on the prevention of murder. After all, even if there were a policeman standing at every doorway in Canada, what is to prevent a desperate husband some night from murdering his wife (or vice versa)?

In contrast, apart from a few incidentals like seat-belt legislation and more parking tickets, the State, servant to the bourgeoisie, closes its eyes to traffic fatalities. This sector may take an alarming number of lives, but it has considerable social clout: 122,816 wounded in 1970 and 416,789 collisions, with more than $100 in damages. In theory, the State controls this entire system which is causing such disaster: public transportation policy, regulations for construction of vehicles, licensing of vehicles, drivers' permits, road networks, highway patrols, etc... But the interests of the giant corporations (the auto industry, oil industry, the entrepreneurs, the insurance companies) do not coincide with the saving of Canadian lives. The State would rather concentrate on those responsible for murder and build more penitentiaries... And enlarge its forces of repression which now add up to some 200,000 people, if you include the police forces (more than 50,000), the army

(78,000) and private security services (*Garda, Citadelle, Canadiana,* etc.) which are estimated to have as many employees as do the police forces.

CHAPTER 5
The Heart of the Matter

Examining the various arguments of the power structure shows us that only political reasons account for the survival and expansion of the penitentiary system: to absorb economic surpluses through the apparatus of repression, a surplus which then makes it possible for more institutions to be built and more jobs created in a sector which reinforces social stability. And, as a side effect, the prison system — through the fear which it causes, through the control which it enforces — permits industry to prosper, for the majority of the population dutifully conform to the status quo. Moreover, there is a glaringly obvious relationship between the GNP (which includes the economic surplus) and the expenditures on the penitentiary system.

TABLE XII

Comparison of possible causes of the growth in expenditures on the canadian penitentiary service and evidence for the theory of the absorption of surpluses

"Overcrowding" Argument	"Rising Crime Rate" Argument	Relationship between the GNP and the Penitentiary System	
2.38%	2.94%	9.65%	16.93%
Average rate of increase in number of inmates in Canadian penitentiaries, 1939-77	Rate of increase in number of people convicted of crimes in Canada, 1949-68	Average rate of annual increase in GNP in Canada, 1946-76	Average rate of annual increase of expenditures by Canadian Penitentiary Service, 1947-77

Absorption of surpluses

Social stability

CHAPTER 6
The Dynamics of Imprisonment

The penitentiary, a political institution, obviously sets off a whole process for the entrenchment of power. This dynamic manifests itself in three ways. First, the sheer physical presence of prisons in the country, a "geopolitical" phenomenon. Second, the act of defining what is to be considered illegal and what is not, which channels popular revolt and limits the threat it poses. Third, the subject matter of this chapter—the extension of repression, as facilitated by the existence of penitentiaries. One way in which this extension takes place is through the development of certain intellectual circles whose role is primarily to legitimize the repression; another is through the development of new techniques of repression which may have direct political application; a third is through increased control and surveillance beyond the institution itself.

The Geopolitical Function

Like most western countries, Canada grew through the geographically expansionist activities of a central government. It is a classic progression—think of the 17th-century unification of France, or the late 19th-century unifications of Germany and Italy. The penitentiary has played an extremely important role in this expansionist process, both as a symbol of the central government and as an expression of the physical presence of its power élite.

In Canada, the penitentiary played a key role in the original four-province Confederation and in subsequent additions to that Confederation. The development of penitentiaries is thus intimately involved with the unification of the country. The 1840 Act of Union of Upper and Lower Canada determined that Kingston was to be the site for a common prison for both provinces. Three years later, a law was passed creating federal-provincial jurisdiction over sentences of two years or more. Confederation, in 1867, divided jurisdictions according to historical precedent and extended administrative control through the dominant position given to the directors of the penitentiaries. In the 1870s, two new provinces entered Confederation and two new penitentiaries were built: Stoney Mountain (1875) in Manitoba, and New Westminster (1878) in British Columbia. In the same decade (in 1873), only six years after the formation of the country, Québec was given its own institution, St. Vincent de Paul.

In 1880, the penitentiaries of St. Jean and Halifax were turned over to the provinces, since a single new penitentiary in New Brunswick, Dorchester, had assumed their former role. It is worth noting that the land on which they were built had been purchased in 1875.

Some years passed before the last two institutions in that first wave of construction opened their doors: Prince Albert, in Saskatchewan, went up in 1911, and Collins Bay, an addition to the Kingston complex, in 1930.

The situation was very similar in the United States — once again, the expansion of the penitentiary system proceeded hand in hand with the unification of the country. It is axiomatic, of course, that integration on that scale could not take place without an equally massive amount of oppression. Just look at the construction dates for penitentiaries in several of the states:

Virginia, 1796; New Jersey, 1798; Kentucky, 1798;

Massachusetts, 1805; Vermont, 1809; Maryland, 1812; Ohio, 1816; Indiana, 1820; New York, 1825; Connecticut, 1827; New Hamsphire, 1832; Maine, 1832; Tennessee, 1833; and so on...

A monotonous list, as it rolls on, and — as in Canada — both a symbol of the power to punish and its physical expression. Amerindians, blacks, the Mexican population, immigrants from the world over, these were the groups which were bent to the will of the bourgeoisie and its State.

Thus, right from the beginning, Canada equipped itself with a nation-wide infrastructure of repression — before it had even thought of setting up institutions of a more social character. We must not underrate the impact of the very existence of a penitentiary in a region, the enormous economic and social polarization that it causes, even to the extent of turning the name of the city itself into a synonym for imprisonment. The very names "Kingston," "St. Vincent de Paul," "Ste. Anne des Plaines," are almost automatically associated with the institutions located there. The penitentiary is an economic magnet, for it is largely staffed with people recruited locally and the physical plant becomes part and parcel of the surroundings, and a service sector springs into being to meet its needs.

The second wave of penitentiary construction may be dated from 1958, but its explosive phase began in 1963 — year one of the ten-year plan and, not coincidentally, the year the Québec independentist movement gained a high profile and the central government felt the need to strengthen its dominant role and bolster national unity.

In only two decades, we went from nine institutions to 55... The trend is certain to continue, for Solicitor-General Francis Fox, in defiance of all logic, trumpets the impending construction of 24 more, eight of them in Québec.

The correlation we are making here may seem exaggerated, in that new institutions are being built all over the country, even though, so far, only Québec has shown secessionist tendencies. But the central government has a clear sense of the possible repercussions of this kind of turmoil. Regional differences are plentiful in Canada, and only one significant group need choose to secede for there to be grave consequences for the whole nation. Take, as an example of this sort of thing, the Basque country in Spain and the repercussions in the Catalan country which threaten the continued existence of that region as a single entity. Or take Bretagne in France, and the effects of that situation in Occitanie and in Corsica. Moreover, though the new penal complexes are a federal political intrusion, their administration has been decentralized, and this has the effect of moderating regional sensitivities. This decentralization also began during the MacLeod régime. Listen to the ex-commissioner's own explanation during his testimony to the MacGuigan sub-committee:

> "We developed the regions because we thought it would assist in the administration of the system generally, once we were getting up to having 30, 35 or 40 institutions... We developed the regions on a modest basis."[73]

Five regional administrative districts were established during the Sixties: Ontario, Québec, the Maritimes, the West, and the Pacific. Prison guards were unionizing at that same time, in the years 1965 and 1966. Obviously, one of the roles of the local authorities would be to serve as a buffer between the institution and the political authorities during work conflicts. But back to the question of regionalization. Commissioner Therrien, while appearing before the sub-committee, provided some interesting details about the process:

> "During the 1960s, following the creation of new institutions and the publication of the Glassco report and the report by the Permanent Committee on Correctional Institutions, the Service began to decentralize administrative functions:
>
> I think, Mr. Chairman, what is happening is that we are in the process of making sure that headquarters is going to get out of operation. We have defined in the first report, which is *Delegation to Regions*, what is precisely the role of headquarters and what is the role of region, what is the role of the institutional level. I think traditionally in headquarters we have been involved in operations — a lot of it — and we are in the process of getting out of it so that there will be only the planning and

control function which will stay in headquarters and more and more of the operational decisions will be taken in the field. That is not something you decide and which happens the next day. It is going to be a long process but we are surely moving in that direction."[74]

There is, of course, a genuine element of "rationalization of management," for the regional level gained responsibilities for such matters as budget and staff management, and the transfer of prisoners. But we should not lose sight of the political dimension. Miliband very accurately described the larger framework for administrative adjustments of this kind:

"In addition to being agents of the state these units of government have also traditionally performed another function. They have not only been the channels of communication and administration from the centre to the periphery, but also the voice of the periphery, or of particular interests at the periphery; they have been a means of overcoming local particularities, but also platforms for their expression, instruments of central control and obstacles to it. For all the centralization of power, which is a major feature of government in these countries, sub-central organs of government, notably in federal systems such as that of the United States, have remained power structures in their own right, and therefore able to affect very markedly the lives of the populations they have governed."[75]

In other words, an event like the seizing of the Bastille had a significance which the chief warden perhaps did not grasp as he watched the crowds closing in on him: they were not attacking the walls of the Bastille, they were attacking the entire power structure!

In an extremely important document entitled *The Social Functions of Prisons in the United States*, the American militant Bettina Aptheker quotes a paragraph by Herbert Marcuse, which beautifully summarizes and explains this whole chapter:

124

"The language of the law and of the present order, articulated by the courts and the police, is not only the voice of oppression, it is, in itself, an act of oppression. This language does not merely define and condemn the Enemy; increasingly, it creates him; and this creation is not that of the Enemy as he is but as he must be in order to carry out his role vis à vis the Establishment."[76]

In his testimony, psychologist Paul Williams of the Correctional Development Centre spoke in much the same way:

"We shall make people who are not dangerous, dangerous, by defining them as such, and we shall make even more dangerous those who are already dangerous by treating them in this way."

Dominated, exploited, oppressed, the people have always rebelled. And their violence often takes a political turn: the occupation of land and later, of factories, the murder of their bosses, the direct appropriation of their milieu, thereby sweeping away parasitic intermediaries.

Every power structure—the feudal lords of the Middle Ages, the monarchies of the *ancien régime* or even the bourgeoisie since the Industrial Revolution—has in turn faced this problem. The various pre-French Revolution powers, vulnerable despite all their advantages, depended primarily for their safety on ideological institutions like the Church, which promised hell-fire in the great beyond to potential rebels and exquisite tortures in the public square to actual and convicted rebels. In other words, they used religious myths to keep the people ignorant and the promise of torture to keep them cowed.

This recipe worked very nicely until the day when the priest, the hangman and the king suddenly found themselves in the public square, this time playing the role of the condemned. The bourgeoisie, as we saw in the section on the history of penitentiaries, drew the appropriate lessons and devised a much more subtle means of controlling popular uprisings. They would not directly confront and suppress

125

revolt; they would channel it into safe directions... safe, at least, for the dominant class.

The system works to define what is "legal" and what is "illegal" at several different levels. For one thing, most people are relatively apolitical, they know little of the basic laws and mechanisms that rule society. This situation is the result of a whole network of factors. The bourgeois institutions of family, school and church take great care during the socialization process *not* to explain the social context in which the child is growing up and the reasons for inequality, misery and oppression. The only values transmitted are those of the bourgeois order, the values of conformity and obedience.

Later, in the workplace, other factors prevent the emergence of class consciousness. The difficulties of uniting and organizing the workers (only 40% of Québec workers are organized or, practically speaking, could be organized), the framework within which this organizing must take place is often hand-in-glove with the existing power structure. The United Steelworkers of America under the leadership of Gérin-Lajoie, or the CLC of Joe Morris, former president of the Canadian Labour Congress are good examples of these collaborationist unions which do nothing to help the workers orient themselves. And finally, of course, there is the betrayal by the élites and the university graduates who, throughout Québec's history, have blocked the emergence of a true political force of the Left. For all these reasons, workers' revolts are focused on goals that do not threaten the authorities and, in the majority of cases, draw public anger on the workers themselves.

The unemployed person who murders the grocer in the corner store... the desperate worker who kills his wife and children... the young worker who uses credit cards for fraudulent purposes or burgles apartments... the unemployed student who starts to push drugs... the man in his fifties who is goaded by the sexual emphasis of the consumer society's advertising to commit rape and sexual assault... What can be said about all these offences, but that they cause few problems on the stock exchanges and never turn into the political revolt that those who commit them — sought to express.

But, the system is already at work.

The sensationalist press labels these people dangerous criminals, and succeeds in alienating them from the rest of the population. The terror begins: police officers systematically use torture during their interrogations; organized fusillades by what can only be called death squads take place outside banks all over the country; judges who gained their positions through patronage hand out exemplary sentences. The holy war to eliminate criminals... exterminate criminals... justifies the budgets, and the repression. The Enemy has been identified; and must be maintained. The penitentiary, in four separate ways, plays a key role in this process. First, it terrorizes the law-abiding majority of the population. The physical fear of imprisonment, the shame, the fear of being thrown in with a dangerous element, the social stigma of having been in the institution, the mystery about what goes on behind the walls, the barbed wire... most people want to avoid ever going through penitentiary gates. This attitude is reinforced by the fact that so many Canadians (75,000 a year, according to figures published by the Law Reform Commission) have the experience of being briefly locked up: overnight in the local drunk tank or three days in a provincial prison for non-payment of fines (half the people in provincial prisons are there for this reason), the victim permanently afraid of the prospect of doing time in a penitentiary.

As a corollary to this first function, the penitentiary experience forever sets the ex-convict apart from the general population.

Now let us look at the various ways in which the penitentiary works upon the people who have been handed over to it. This, of course, brings us to the subjects of the classification system applied to prisoners and the types of institutions to be found within the Canadian penitentiary system. The criteria for the classification of prisoners have never been precisely defined. Criminologist Claude Gaulin, in his 1972 thesis, attempted to sort out the evidence.[77]

When the prisoner, at the beginning of a sentence, arrives at the classification centre (the Regional Reception Centre in Québec, in the Ste. Anne des Plaines complex), the documentation usually consists of the following:

1. a judicial file;

2. the police report (the offence, attitude at the time of arrest and during the interrogation, etc.); and

3. the pre-sentencing report, should one exist (psychological or psychiatric).

According to Gaulin, there are three methods for classifying the prisoner. The most common is to equate the criminal with the criminal act. The second is based on personality type. This is the most psychologically-oriented of the classification systems. It is structured in terms of "motivational patterns," which are a combination of the personality type and various psychological states according to which crime "is seen as a symptomatic product of underlying mental conditions." The third system is based on life-style: professional criminals, accidental criminals, habitual criminals, etc.

In general, the classification officer uses the results of all three approaches in order to decide upon the appropriate institution for the prisoner. But all this is incidental: since the reception centres have in fact quite another role to play. They and their classification files are there to demonstrate institutional power over the inmate.

Basically, there are three types of penitentiary institutions in Canada: maximum, medium and minimum security. In addition, there are transition centres and super-maximum institutions.

We have seen in our historical review that this system of divisions was born during the MacLeod régime. Here is how this reform came about:

"The maximum security institution was one where the worst and most dangerous offenders were to be confined. They were inmates who were regarded as being likely to make active efforts to escape and could very well be dangerous to the community if they did escape. Our calculation at that time was that some 35 per cent of the inmate population fell into that category.

Fifty per cent of the inmate population, we thought, could be classified as medium security, people who were not likely to make active efforts to escape, who might take advantage of the open door, if they found an open door, but were not likely to be dangerous to the community if they did go through that door."[78]

We have reviewed the selection criteria, and seen that the factor given the most weight seemed to be the "dangerosity" of the criminal, especially in combination with the crime that had been committed; we have seen that, according to MacLeod's testimony, the major criterion for the classification of institutions was the degree of possibility of escape from them. Now let us look at the types of "criminals" sent to the institutions... in other words, let us examine the profile of the 1976 penitentiary population.

TABLE XIII
Serious offences[79]

Murder, attempted murder and involuntary homicide	1,401	15.3%
Dangerous sexual offenders, rape and other sexual offences	700	7.7%
Assault, attempted robbery or robbery	2,995	32.7%
Drugs	911	9.9%
Breaking and entry, theft or resale of stolen objects	1,976	21.6%
Fraud	415	4.5%
Other	759	8.3%
Total	9,158	100%

Finally, let us look at what kind of institution these people are sent to:

TABLE XIV
Distribution of prisoner by degree of security of penitentiary, end of 1976[80]

Maximum security	3,775	40.4%
Medium security	4,364	46.7%
Minimum security	1,205	12.9%

The data calls for certain observations.

For one thing, maximum-security institutions in fact receive a higher percentage of prisoners than the MacLeod plan has foreseen: 40.4% of the population, instead of 35 per cent. There is, in other words, a tendency for the penitentiaries to stress security measures, and thus, to stress more repression for more people. The MacGuigan report made much of this phenomenon:

> "Since the overcrowding is particularly serious in medium security institutions, there are a large number of inmates presently in maximum security who would, under normal circumstances, be in medium security... It is clear that there is a bottleneck in the system when minimum security institutions are actually operating below their capacity while maximum and medium security institutions are overcrowded."[81]

The report then attempts to justify the situations:

> "The problem may result from the historical context in which maximum security was until recently the normal disposition of a person sentenced to imprisonment. Classification practice may not yet have fully adjusted itself to the innovations of medium and minimum security."[82]

The maximum-security penitentiary not only holds more and more prisoners, it also has considerable impact on the medium-security prison. In fact, "medium security" institutions are acquiring more and more of the attributes of the maximum-security penitentiaries: peepholes, internal discipline, armed guards.

When you look at the offences which have been committed by the prisoners (Table XIII), you see that 23% of them are listed as "dangerous." Note, however, that the State includes in this category involuntary homicide, murder and sexual offences (which may amount to nothing more than offences against modesty). The tactic serves to inflate the statistics, a very effective way to inflate the percentage of "dangerous criminals." It was logical for MacLeod to stress the danger of escape as the main criterion for penitentiary categories but, even so, the nature of the offence committed by the prisoner surely plays some role in determining to which institution that person is sent. However, since there is a dearth of dangerous criminals, the pretext of escape (and what prisoner would not want to escape?) provides the ideal excuse for increased security. Moreover, several witnesses suggested that the number of "dangerous" prisoners is in fact much smaller — at least, when they *enter* the penitentiaries — than the statistical breakdown would indicate.

Consider the words of Mr. Murphy, regional director for the Pacific, during his testimony to the sub-committee:

> "The bulk of the inmates are not destructive, violent people, but we have among the inmate population a number of people who are violent, who are destructive."[83]

And Mr. Twyman, regional vice-president of the P.S.A.C.:

> "I believe if you take the 9,000 inmates that we have in Canada that there is a small percentage which has to be locked up."[84]

And finally, the words of the commissioner of penitentiaries himself, who went even farther than the others in estimating the size of the discrepancy between the number of "dangerous" criminals and the number of people being held in maximum-security institutions:

"I don't believe we do much about the subject of those who are inclined to violence, for example, and they represent 15% of the total population."[85]

The conclusions are inescapable: 15% of prisoners, they claim, are dangerous, but 87.1% are locked up in conditions of extreme security, or conditions tending that way, given the trend in "medium" security institutions.

Why? The effects of imprisonment give us the answer.

The penitentiary, a breeding ground for criminals, helps maintain this "offender" category, this group of marginalized human beings who pose no threat to the power structure and in fact contribute to the stability of the régime's system of repression. In the words of former solicitor-general Warren Allmand:

"The majority of offenders serving sentences for breaking and entering, theft and fraud, have previously been imprisoned."[86]

The penitentiary is a meeting place for apprenticeship in criminal techniques; it causes many to turn to larceny as a means of survival or as an expression of revolt against the conditions of oppression in which they find themselves. The great majority of prisoners are predestined for a very specialized function within the system:

"Eighty per cent of offenders have been at liberty for less than 18 months after completing a previous term of imprisonment."[87]

For these people, crime and penitentiary become the normal, repeated zig-zag of their lives. The system can easily control the oscillation — and, as we have already seen, this phenomenon has, from the bourgeois point of view, attractive side effects as far as general social control is concerned.

One may say that about 80% of all prisoners join this closed circle for good. They are fulfilling a role which has been created for them by the penitentiary system itself.

A second category of prisoner is physically and/or psychologically destroyed by the penal machine. The dreadful conditions of imprisonment result, for some, in suicide, the settling of accounts, self-mutilations, nervous disorders, and murder. This role, too, has been planned and is maintained by the system. Terror, even on a limited scale, is one way to make the rest of the population fear the punishments decreed by the judiciary. Media coverage, reports, and personal testimonies are enough to keep most people on the straight-and-narrow. The rule of fear has always been an extremely effective way for one class to dominate another.

Finally, the penitentiary transforms some people — but once again, we are speaking of a very small percentage of the prison population — into serious threats to the community. This function, too, is the result of imprisonment and, precisely because it is on a small scale, helps the system justify increased repression. It is in this group that we find the "Richard Blasses" and the "Léopold Dions," who have been so affected by prison repression that they have become extremely hostile to the outside world and whenever they are in it — whether during a prison break or upon being set free — spread terror.

The phenomenon of increased aggressivity as a result of incarceration is corroborated by numerous witnesses:

> "I was put in a position in 1970 where it was either a case of having a nervous breakdown or killing myself or taking a hostage, so I chose to take the hostage. Sometimes, under such circumstances, you are not responsible." (a prisoner)[88]

Note that prisoners of this kind are all from penitentiaries. André Therrien:

> "One must emphasize that few prisoners are always, or even always potentially, violent. Violence is a function of personality traits in reaction to a particular situation, and we must admit that some conditions in the institutions increase the tendency to violence in certain persons. The mere fact of incarceration in a maximum security institution may provoke a behaviour pattern which bears out the implications of the expression "maximum security'."[89]

In conclusion, we may state that the consequences of imprisonment are those which the system desires. The maintenance of a category of the population labelled "criminal," the physical and/or psychological and social destruction of another segment of the population, the marked increase in aggressivity among certain individuals (who give the word "danger" its meaning), the maintenance of the fear of punishment among the population as a whole—these things permit the power structure to perpetuate itself and to regulate social control.

The Refinement and Expansion of Repression

Finally, the penal dynamic expresses itself in the refinement of techniques of repression, and in their expansion through subtle forms of surveillance and control beyond penitentiary walls. Let us start by examining how the prison encourages torture groups on the inside.

The Creation of Torturers

Perhaps the most sadistic aspect of the penitentiary system is that it turns an entire category of workers against prisoners by subjecting them as well to the evil effects of imprisonment. For the prisoners are not alone in their situation: the system so arranges things that the guards, who have a certain amount of discretionary power over prisoners, also fall victim to the heightened aggressivity caused by imprisonment and are then allowed to work off this aggression on the prisoners. The process is quite simple. First, legislation ensures that this category of worker may not make common cause in a true, combative workers' trade union. (That is, correctional agents are cut off as much as possible from the working class as a whole, and devote themselves entirely to the service of the bourgeois State.)

Recommendation 27 of the MacGuigan report lays down terms for the unionization of prison guards:

> "Employees of the Penitentiary Service who perform supervisory or confidential functions should not be entitled to belong to unions."[90]

The consequences of this kind of class isolation are a generalized withdrawal, the development of a very strong group ethos and suspicion about any progressive ideas. It causes them to take extremely reactionary positions and, finally, it causes widespread feelings of persecution and of being misunderstood by other social groups. Is it not always the guards who call for the return to corporal punishment, the re-introduction of capital punishment and harsh measures against the prisoners?

The authorities of the State are well aware of this process, and use it to their own ends. (Though, of course, the authorities reserve the right to slash personnel, freeze pay hikes, adversely affect working conditions and set themselves up as arbitrators when the guards go a little too far in the line of duty.) By forcing the guards into conditions of imprisonment as well, the State is guilty of indirect physical violence against the prisoners, for the State knows the effects of imprisonment. And so, inmates are beaten with iron bars in New Westminster, other captives are chained and clubbed in Millhaven, mad gassings take place in the Correctional Development Centre... no matter. The prisoners must feel in their own flesh the strength of the power structure.

And when it is time for a major inquiry, for the periodic housecleaning, then the government causes a few administrative heads to roll, refurbishes the image of the correctional service and finds a few scapegoats among its employees, but the basic evil is untouched. Imprisonment will continue to mould the guards, since a position of authority in a totalitarian institution causes any group, whatever group it may be, to develop an identically brutal pattern of behaviour. Even if, as has been recommended, new guards must satisfy higher educational requirements and take a three-month course, even if guards are made to wear name tags, absolutely nothing will change.

Two university experiments carried out by Zimbardo[91] and Milgram[92] are dramatic proof of our argument.

A professor of psychology at the University of Stanford in California, Philip Zimbardo, undertook an experiment to demonstrate the effects of imprisonment on volunteer subjects. For this purpose, a windowless prison was created, complete with cells, iron doors, and a "hole"—in short, an anonymous, dehumanizing place. A newspaper advertisement recruited volunteers for the experiment.

Twenty subjects were finally chosen from the seventy-five candidates, all of them in their twenties, psychologically and physically well-balanced, and well-educated. The roles of guard and prisoner were distributed at random. The ten men chosen to be prisoners temporarily gave up their civil rights. They were dressed in a white shirt, without underclothes, their heads covered with a nylon hood and their personal belongings taken away from them. The clothing gave them an extremely feminine appearance and restricted their movements. Thereafter they were known only by their identification numbers.

The "guards" were just as depersonalized. They all wore the same khaki uniform, mirrored sunglasses that hid their eyes and they were given the usual equipment: whistles, billy-clubs, handcuffs and rings of keys.

The prisoners had to obey a list of regulations and ask permission for even trivial activities: to smoke, to write, to go to the bathroom. The guards were allowed to make up new prisoner-control strategies of management and to use their powers in arbitrary fashion.

The experiment was meant to last fifteen days but had to be stopped after six, so badly had the situation deteriorated. The "guards" used every possible means of degrading and demoralizing the "prisoners." The "prisoners" reacted with rebellion, by escape attempts, and utter passivity. They came to think only of food and flight. "We could no longer tell," said Professor Zimbardo, "where reality began and where the role-playing left off."

The prisoners very quickly developed physical and psychological problems. Outbursts of tears and of rage were frequent. The guards frequently abused their authority, even torturing the prisoners physically.

A very strong group spirit developed among the guards. They accused those of their group who were not taking maximum advantage of their position of being "weak," or of "playing the prisoners' game." The "goods guards" were few in number. The psychologist quickly concluded that "individual behaviour is largely determined by exterior social forces or by the demands of the environment."

A guard who testified before the sub-committee was therefore right when he said:

> "I have worked in minimum, medium and maximum security institutions for ten years, and it makes you bad-tempered and suspicious of practically everybody."

The Milgram experiment, which took place at Harvard in the United States, shows just how far individuals such as guards or police, who work in an authoritarian atmosphere, will go in carrying out appalling orders unquestioningly. The phenomenon is even more pronounced in a totalitarian institution like the penitentiary.

This experiment was carried out in the following way.

Some people, recruited once again through newspaper advertisements, came to a psychology laboratory which purported to be carrying out research into memory and learning. They were divided into the two groups of "monitors" and "students." The experimenter explained that they wished to study the effects of punishment on the learning process. He took the student (who had been let in on the deception) into a separate room, installed him in a chair equipped with restraining straps, and attached an electrode to the candidate's finger. The student, so the fiction went (but the monitor did not know it was fiction), was being required to learn a list of word-pairings. Every time he had a mistake, he received (supposedly) an electric shock, each shock stronger than the last. Since the monitor was unaware that the student's behaviour, the electric shocks and the learning process were all a deception, the true subject of the experiment was in fact the monitor's behaviour, faced with the actions and responses of the student. The purpose of the experiment was to discover how long an individual in a concrete and measurable situation would obey orders to inflict increasingly severe punishments on a victim who protested violently all the while, and at what moment the subject would refuse to obey the experimenter's orders any longer.

This experiment, through the newspaper advertisements, drew on a broad base. The chosen subjects were carefully balanced by age and occupation: the subjects for each experiment (for the experiment was repeated many times, each time with several different variables) were 40% skilled and unskilled workers, 40% office workers, salesmen and businessmen, and 20% functionaries. Twenty per cent of the participants in each experiment were in their twenties, 30% were in their thirties and forties, and 40% were older. Men and women alike were chosen.

The psychiatrists based their expectations of their subjects' behaviour on the following assumptions:

a. generally speaking, people are relatively good and not inclined to cause the innocent to suffer; and

b. in the absence of physical coercion or the threat of such coercion, the individual is absolute master of his own conduct, and will act in a given manner because he has chosen to do so.

What the experiment in fact clearly demonstrated was that, placed in a position of obedience to an authority believed to be legitimate, the great majority of the "monitors" administered the "electric shock" to the backward "students," even when they knew that the "shocks" had reached potentially fatal levels of intensity. The majority (more than 60%) never questioned the justification for such a procedure.

Adults, in other words, have an overwhelming tendency to submit almost unconditionally to orders from authority figures. In our social system, obedience is the psychological mechanism which integrates individual action with the political grand plan, the natural cement binding people to authority systems.

The same experiment was tried in the Max Plank Institute in the German Federal Republic, with the same results.

So one must not be too surprised that guards show no particular reaction to the conditions of prisoners in the maximum-security institutions (often 24 hours a day in the cell, gassings, etc.): placed in this totalitarian system and conditioned by the media and the contents of the criminals' dossiers, they believe it legitimate to punish, to chastize, the prisoners.

The system thus creates a group of torturers who are entirely devoted to that system.

Support From The Professionals: The Special Correctional Unit

The system of repression in the prisons is not limited to goon squads who physically harass and brutalize the prisoners. The system also sets up pilot institutions to refine procedures for destroying the prisoners, procedures above and beyond those already mentioned (violation of rights, isolation, etc.) and in use throughout the system. Professionals of every kind (architects, criminologists, psychologists) have been given a free hand to design and perpetuate what is undoubtedly the worst institution yet to see the light of day in Canada, or all North America, for that matter. It is therefore important to trace the history of this institution, especially since it is not an aberration, but rather the prototype for the 24 new establishments which, according to Solicitor-General Francis Fox's recent announcement, are to be built over the next five years. These institutions will provide accommodation for a limited number of people, but each one of them will receive a great deal of attention.

The many professionals who fought the establishment of this kind of institution will find this claim exaggerated. But many others co-operated whole-heartedly—if discreetly.

During the famous MacLeod reform era of the Sixties, it was announced that four prototype institutions, to be called "Special Detention Units," were to be constructed. They were to hold those prisoners whom the American Manual of Correctional Standards designated as: "incorrigible, intractable and dangerous."[93]

Only one, however, was built—in Québec.

In 1965, a contract in the amount of $2,362,600 was awarded to Vermont Construction Inc. of Montréal, for the construction of a "super," as it was called by the prisoners. The

139

plans and drawings had been jointly prepared by the Ministry of Public Works and S.-A. Cyr, a Montréal architectural consultant. The State and private enterprise, after all, have always co-operated in the fight to suppress workers...

Controversy began as soon as the plan to construct these ultra/maximum-security units was announced. Organizations like the League of Human Rights, the John Howard Society, the Forensic Clinic, well aware of the danger posed by such plans, demanded an immediate halt to the project. One of the opponents of the scheme, Bruno Cormier, drew on his pioneering experience in psychiatric work with the Canadian Penitentiary Service itself in his scathing attack on the project. According to him, the institution would lead to an escalation of violence among the prisoners, driving them to "more, and more serious, crimes." Prophetic words: Richard Blass, who had been held in the Special Correctional Unit, hit the headlines when he went on a murder spree unprecedented in Québec history.

Cormier put it this way:

> "What happens in such cases is that, finally, the inmates' defence mechanisms rebound on them and they refuse to leave their cells; then, when they are sent back into society, they are completely incapable of adapting to it."[94]

But the project found its defenders, invariably from within the Canadian Penitentiary Service. Michel Le Corre, for example — a former member of the French navy and later director of St. Vincent de Paul, who gained notoriety during a 1963 hostage-taking incident at that institution (when he ordered guards to fire on a prisoner, thereby causing the death of the captive guard — Le Corre said he was amazed by the opposition to the project, and then offered this justification for it:

> "1. The cells of the Special Unit are lit by a window into the roof. It is therefore false to claim that the inmates will live in utter blackness.
>
> 2. It is false to say that the inmates will be deprived of human sensory qualities because the cells are too thoroughly sealed. The best

proof I can offer of the falsity of this charge is that the system will allow us to pipe radio broadcasts into each of the cells.

3. It is also false to claim that the inmates will lose all contact with the guards, since there will effectively be contact every time the prisoner is called to come out of his cell, and this will happen a number of times every day.

4. ...a training programme will be in effect in the special units which will allow the prisoners to take advantage of educational courses, to work, to follow a physical fitness programme. Moreover, each one of them will have personal responsibility for the cleaning of his room and the care of his own clothing."[95]

M. Le Corre's eloquence helped boost him a few steps up the hierarchical ladder. In 1977, he became head of the Québec Region of the Canadian Penitentiary Service.

Politicians jumped into the fray. Guy Favreau, then minister of justice in the Pearson cabinet, told the media that he would consider the possibility of delaying construction until a study of the question could be carried out by a parliamentary committee (August 6, 1965). His successor, Cardin, also said he would study the problem...

In 1968, the Special Detention Unit opened its doors. It came in seriously over budget, for costs had risen to a final total of $7 million. M. Le Corre was that same year named director of the New Ste. Anne des Plaines institution... far away from the SDU cells and their radio broadcasts.

The purpose of the institutions was clear: according to the authorities, the SDU was to hold those people who required more stringent control than that which could be enforced in a normal maximum-security institution. Its capacity was 140 prisoners — an estimated 3% or 4% of the total prison population, the toughest and most dangerous of them all.

The Special Detention Unit has had three directors to date : Roger Jourdain, 1968-69; Jean Pagé, 1969-71; and finally, Pierre Goulem from 1971 on.

Those three men may fairly be called the "intellectuals" of the Canadian Penitentiary Service. According to the MacGuigan report, it was their intention to set up an "active, committed" therapeutic group within the establishment.

Meanwhile, prisoners delivered their own judgment on the SDU. Or, some of them did—on July 7, 1969, Gordon Garraghty, Claude Martin and Paul Mikulis escaped from this supposedly "ultra-security" institution.

Conditions there were appalling. In their efforts to break the prisoners' spirits, the authorities used the same programmes as in most other penitentiaries, but in an intensified form. Even the most trivial aspects of daily life were subjected to a systematic punishment/privilege framework. It is well worth quoting this pilot-programme in full, for the endless provocations and the endless battles for even the tiniest of improvements that it reveals are deliberate and desired parts of the Canadian Penitentiary Service régime.

The Special Correctional Centre consists of four buildings, each housing one category of the Centre's prisoner population, corresponding to one of the four stages of the overall correctional programme.

The goal of the programme is to effect a change in the prisoner's social attitude and sense of responsibility so that, as soon as possible, this person may be returned to a "normal" institution.

However, before that can take place, the prisoner must demonstrate a real change in attitudes and behaviour, and show enough interest in normal institutional life to wish to participate in training programmes.

It must be understood that the primary objective of the correctional programme of the Special Correctional Unit *is to correct and not to punish.*

However, since the maintenance of order is essential for the effective operation of any educational institution, the prisoners will be under close supervision so as to prevent the repetition of the anti-social, anti-human or anti-institutional acts that these people may have previously committed.

Therefore, discipline will be strict, it will be applied consistently and fairly, and its severity will vary appropri-

142

ately with the circumstances of the person in question.

Immediate prevention of anti-social behaviour, however, is not the only goal of the disciplinary régime. It must be interpreted and focused in such a way as to lead the prisoners to assume full responsibility for their own actions, to accept institutional discipline as an essential step toward eventual self-discipline and to realize that self-discipline is an essential condition for a healthy and balanced life, whether in an institution or not.

Disciplinary restrictions will therefore be those judged capable of protecting society and the Centre's staff, as well as the prisoners themselves.

N.B. The non-adherents' programme is designed for the prisoners who are following a policy of total non-cooperation — who reject any contact with the therapeutic personnel and who, right from the beginning, systematically refuse to participate in the graduated correctional programme. The work assignments and physical activities of the non-participants will resemble closely those for stage 1 of the participants' programme. Privileges, however, will be reduced to the bare minimum and there will be no possibility of returning to a normal institution, since the necessary condition for that return is to have successfully gone through all the stages of the graduated correctional programme.

Stage 1 - Isolation

This initial period must be long enough to allow time for the officials responsible for the evaluation and orientation period, and the various rehabilitation specialists, to evaluate the potential of the prisoners in question and to put them through an orientation session. This isolation stage facilitates contact between the officials and the prisoner since the prisoner is not being negatively influenced by the presence of other prisoners. This, therefore, is the most favourable moment for the system to attempt to influence the prisoner, but also the most delicate, and the one which demands the greatest degree of tact and diplomacy on the part of the officials. Their ability to establish good relations with the prisoner in this stage will determine future attitudes to authority and to the programme. This is, therefore, the most important stage of the entire graduated correctional programme.

Austerity vs. Education

The austerity which is enforced during this first stage is not for punishment purposes. Rather, it is to encourage the prisoner to participate in the programme as soon as possible so as to win the additional privileges incorporated into each subsequent stage. It also serves as a warning and a back-up for those who have graduated to succeeding stages, for those who have been returned to maximum-security institutions, and in general for all prisoners in all penal institutions.

The main purpose of the deprivations in this first stage is to facilitate teaching the prisoner to make a personal effort, through the practice of self-discipline (which is at the base of responsible behaviour, whether in society or in an institution). Since sustained personal effort is the price of success in education, it must be at the heart of our system. However, this educational process cannot take place until the prisoner decides to co-operate with it. The formidable challenge faced by the institution's training personnel is to win the prisoner's co-operation, for it is only when the system *is accepted* by the prisoner that *its application* during a *sufficiently lengthy* period of time may train their will and teach them to control themselves so that, in the future, they will be better able to handle the inevitable frustrations of life in a penal institution. In other words, learning to discipline themselves in their routine daily activities will help them discipline themselves that much better in the larger effort. But even if *a priori* it seems that the planned programme of austerity will lead the individual to co-operate with the programme, one must remember that effort and interest do not necessarily exclude each other, although a system of effort and a system of will may exclude each other. The system, therefore, must combine the two elements: on the one hand, the prisoner must clearly see where their immediate interest lies and, on the other, they must see the effort which they must voluntarily make in order

144

to obtain satisfaction. From all the evidence, a large part of the success of a programme of this type lies in the way in which it is "sold" by the officials during the indoctrination period. It is crucial that it is presented in such a way as to cause the prisoner to have a positive attitude about the challenge which this programme presents.

First, they must be led to see themselves clearly, to understand that they have chosen the wrong path, to grasp that out of their own self-interest they must make an *effort* to work, to strengthen their personality so as to give themselves maximum opportunities for happiness in life. One must never take the attitude: "Poor man, it's not your fault, you couldn't help it!" Only society's cast-offs, true idiots and imbeciles, should be treated in this way.

However, it must here be repeated that *the basic criterion is that the individual accept the régime*, and it is that which is the *challenge* faced by the personnel running the indoctrination stage. It is absolutely essential that the prisoners admitted to the Special Correctional Centre *are led to accept* the programme.

If we succeed in inculcating among our prisoners the sense of effort, in directing their energies and cultivating their will, we shall be pleasantly surprised by the academic and vocational possibilities that they then reveal.

Privileges Granted In Stage 1

1. 1 letter a week (to an approved person)
2. 2 monthly visits (30 min.) (approved person)
3. educational books
4. restricted smoking
5. no association with others
6. salary (group 1 only)
7. radio, per the established schedule

Privileges To Be Acquired

1. normal association with other inmates
2. unrestricted smoking
3. subscriptions to magazines and newspapers
4. canteen
5. visits and correspondence (regular and special privilege)
6. library (regular withdrawal of books)
7. sports and recreational activities
8. radio (extra privileges)
9. movies
10. group work
11. hobbies
12. regular socio-cultural activities
13. change of institution

Privileges Granted In Stage II

1. smoking (acquired privilege)
2. sending of 1 letter a week
3. two monthly visits; unlimited receiving of correspondence from authorized persons
4. library (acquired privilege)
5. socio-cultural activities (restricted)
6. salary (group 1)
7. radio, per the established schedule (acquired privilege)

Privileges To Be Acquired

1. normal association
2. subscriptions — magazines and newspapers
3. smoking (normal privilege)

4. canteen
5. regular and special visits and correspondence
6. library (regular privilege)
7. recreation and sports (indoors and outdoors)
8. radio (acquired privilege)
9. movies
10. regular group work
11. hobbies
12. normal socio-cultural privileges
13. transfer to other institutions

Privileges Granted In Stage III

1. restricted association
2. unrestricted smoking
3. subscription to a weekly newspaper
4. regular visits and correspondence
5. library (regular withdrawal of books)
6. radio, per accepted schedule
7. group work (restricted)
8. hobbies
9. socio-cultural activities

Privileges To Be Won

1. normal association
2. magazine subscriptions
3. canteen
4. library
5. sporting and recreational activities (indoors and outdoors)
6. radio and TV
7. movies
8. group work

9. transfer to another institution

Privileges Granted In Stage IV

1. normal association with other inmates
2. salary for group 1
3. library
4. radio
5. smoking (regular privilege)
6. subscriptions: papers: 1 daily, 1 weekly
   magazines: 1 (from approved list)
7. canteen
8. regular and special visits and correspondence
9. regular library use
10. sporting and recreational activities, indoors and outdoors
11. movies (twice monthly, from a selected list)
12. hobbies
13. socio-cultural activities
14. workshop activities
15. academic courses

Privileges To Be Acquired

Transfer to another institution

The programme for *non-participants* will be divided into two phases:

Phase "A": Includes all the activities and privileges of stage 1, except for interviews with training personnel.
No association among inmates will be tolerated and they will UNDER ALL CIRCUMSTANCES be escorted everywhere by two correctional officers.

In this phase will be found all new arrivals who refuse to participate in the regular programme, and those inmates from stages 2, 3 or 4 who, because of unsatisfactory progress and lack of co-operation have been, after individual review by the classification committee or the superintendent, removed from these stages.

Any new arrival in this phase who decides to participate in the programme will OBLIGATORILY be assigned to stage 1.

Phase "B":   Includes the following activities:
- daily half-hour walk in the yard, weather permitting;
- cleaning his cell,
- daily shower,
- privileges: none.

The inmates must at all times be escorted by two guards.

To this phase will be assigned those inmates from phase "A" who refuse to participate in the activities of that phase.

Phase "B" inmates must go through phase "A" before being eligible for the graduated correctional programme.

The architecture of the buildings was modelled on the findings of research conducted by D. Hebb of McGill University, a world authority on the subject of sensory deprivation — who, it must be made clear, has never pursued his work for repressive purposes.

Disputes arose between the administration of the institution and the regional Québec administration over programme content. One director succeeded another. But those people — including some prisoners — who interpreted the directors' position as a highly progressive one were mistaken. Even if the kind of psychologically-based programme which they wished to establish was less blatant than that favoured by the "old guard," it was just as formidable. In fact, it was more

149

so, for instead of torturing the prisoner's body, it worked on the brain, seeking to dissolve the personality, to shatter defences. Two spectacular escapes took place during Pierre Goulem's time, causing the "criminologist" director's demotion and the temporary shutting down of the Centre (from 1973 to 1974).

Public opinion was also aroused by the systematic use of gas on the institution's prisoners. An assistant-director, Laval Grondon, gave practical demosntrations on prisoners who were locked in their cells, and usually sent a letter to a prisoner who had been punished which explained that suffering would allow prisoners to redeem themselves. Grondon now holds an important position in the Leclerc institution.

On August 22, 1972, Jean-Paul Mercier, Jacques Masrine, Pierre Vincent, Robert Imbeault, André Ouellet and Michel Lafleur managed to escape after two years in what one *La Presse* journalist called the "Canadian Alcatraz." Goulem, forgetting everything he had learned in his psychology courses at the Université de Montréal, commented on the event in these words:

> "The prisoners who are held there are vicious men who have absolutely no scruples about violence."[96]

To add insult to injury, there were, at the time, 65 guards for some 15 prisoners.

During the year which separated this second escape from the one which had (temporarily) closed the institution, a number of intellectuals became involved in a celebrated effort to transform the institution into a pilot project in subtle and insidious repression. Aubert Laferrière, regional director at the time, told the media that the ultra-maximum institution would soon have an entirely new orientation. The subject of the press conference was a three-volume confidential report prepared by a psychiatrist for the solicitor-general on the treatment of prisoners and the training of personnel. The intended future programme for the Special Correctional Centre would be designed to experiment with rehabilitation methods for a selected group of prisoners. Great emphasis was placed on the importance of bringing together a multi-disciplinary team.

Laferrière concluded his explanations with the words:

"We have the master plan. Now we must find a way to apply it."

The treatment programme fascinated and tempted intellectuals, for it offered them the opportunity to test their theories at last. Criminologist M. A. Bertrand, who later became infamous for his stand on the legalization of marijuana while a member of the Le Dain Commission, had a few thoughts on the subject:

> "If Mr. Goyer [solicitor-general at the time], when he talks about rehabilitation and treatment, is talking about what scientific individuals think of as a therapeutic environment capable of modifying the behaviour of individuals who are imprisoned there, this environment demands a hand-picked staff able to change the values and objectives of criminals."[97]

The psychiatrist who spent the summer of 1971 writing the explosive report was Bruno Cormier, and he drew very negative conclusions about the institution.

Physical conditions were deplorable (ventilation, sensory deprivation, artificial light); psychological and physiological degradation were both very pronounced. The kind of suppression being practised there (repeated gassings, torture) had serious consequences: numerous self-mutilations, suicide attempts, mental deterioration of the captives. Director Goulem retorted: "Some inmates attempt suicide just to give the institution a bad reputation."[98]

After the report was submitted to the solicitor-general in January of 1972, psychologist André Thiffault (then head of the service at the Philippe-Pinel Institute) was approached and asked to get the new therapeutic committee on its feet. The other members of the group were: André Normandeau, director of the department of criminology at the Université de Montréal; Marcel Frechette, criminologist; Paul Williams, psychologist; Mrs. Maryrose Lette, now a member of the Parole Board; and Michel Le Corre, whose radio broadcasts into the CDC cells didn't seem to have given the desired results. The group's mandate was to define more precise and practicable goals. (In university jargon, this kind of formula means a great deal.)

151

The central purpose of all this discussion and activity was to pull together an interdisciplinary team, supported by the Université de Montréal every step of the way, to run a programme at the Special Correctional Centre for the resocialization of adult criminals. In summary:

1. To plan, organize and administer a new kind of detention centre for adult criminal recidivists;
2. To neutralize extremely dangerous individuals through a combination of adequate security and a programme of reintegration;
3. Moreover, this programme for hardened criminals would be of interest to the entire penitentiary system; and
4. The internalization by the inmate, as a service to society, of his social responsibilities.

The Thiffault report, however, contradicted the Cormier recommendations. Cormier proposed that the Special Correctional Unit become a pre-liberation centre for 120 prisoners who presented special evaluation difficulties as parole candidates — for example, frequent recidivists who had personality problems, were likely to learn from experience, aged 20-30 and eligible for parole within a period of 18-24 months; or some occasional prisoners who had committed such grave offences that they required in-depth evaluation before being granted parole; or, finally, prisoners who had served long sentences and were very profoundly institutionalized. The Cormier plan wanted to exclude prisoners who were considered serious disciplinary problems and lacked motivation to take part in the programme.

The Thiffault group, in contrast, insisted that the Special Correctional Unit remain what it already was, a maximum-security experimental centre, and that it not become a pre-liberation centre. The Thiffault version of how to "treat" incorrigibles obviously stood a good chance of being accepted by the Canadian Penitentiary Service and the politicians, given the extremely repressive purpose which it was intended to serve.

The Cormier model for the therapeutic community was at least based on the voluntary consent of the prisoner, and had as its objective to accelerate the liberation process. The objectives of the Thiffault group, however, were fascist in nature and unacceptable on every point. They were calling on the techniques of the human sciences, not to help individuals but to destroy their personalities, to break them down. Under these circumstances, every critical remark they might draw out of prisoners, thoughts they might have about the authorities but would normally keep to themselves, would be used against them. The Thiffault group, for all its "professional" and "humanizing" veneer, did not intend to help people develop; the goal was to manipulate them in order to oppress them even more.

As expected, the State gave the nod to the Thiffault group's report, and confirmed it in March of 1972 with a third study group. This time, they called upon "professionals" already working for the Canadian Penitentiary Service. The guidelines for the ultra-maximum were drawn up under the direction of R. Jourdain (first director of the Special Correctional Centre) by Messrs. Bisson (psychiatrist with the regional medical centre), Goulem (director of the SCC), Grondon ("gas expert" and attached to the classification section of the SCU), and Marineau (director of the Archambeault institution and today in charge of regional security):

1. The SCU was no longer to serve as a detention centre for "trouble-makers" from other institutions. It was to become a regional experimental maximum-security centre where a new programme would be tested with selected groups of inmates (those who posed a danger to the personnel; who were likely to attempt escape; murderers; violent criminals; agitators; individuals who needed protection, etc.);

2. The name of the institution was to be changed so as to erase the stigma attached to the old name;

3. Production lines would be established (in wood- or metal-working) and workshops for crafts and repair work as well, given the proven therapeutic values of these occupations. To these activities would be added the maintenance and repair work for the institution itself, and academic classes;

153

4. There would be the systematic use of group therapy techniques; and

5. No physical alterations to the buildings would be necessary. The existing infirmary was adequate, and the Catholic chapel, appropriate. No change to the cells seemed necessary at that time.

The Jourdain committee, however, felt the need to counter the extremely negative remarks made about the cells by Dr. Cormier, and so called on the SCU psychiatrist, Dr. Voyer. Here is what he had to say:

> "The charge that these cells dehumanize the inmate, which has been levelled by certain behavioural scientists, is without foundation. The inmates themselves only talk about their cells when newspapers stir up a fuss about them and, even then, their comments are trivial. Life in this cell is no more prejudicial to the personality of the inmate than life in any other cell. No mental or emotional pathology has developed, or worsened, because of the physical characteristics of the cell."[99]

We shall have more to say about the sensory deprivation caused by this kind of building—very similar results, according to the specialists, to those obtained by Hebb during his experiments.

In September 1972, the solicitor-general deemed himself satisfied by the stack of files which effectively justified Canadian Penitentiary Service policies, and accepted the conclusions of the report. Specialists were accordingly hired, and Director Goulem supervised the construction of two common rooms and five offices.

In January 1973, the special correctional unit officially became the Correctional Development Centre (CDC). Psychologists Thiffault and Williams were named assistants to the director. The Université de Montréal seconded a researcher, Pierre Lagier, to the project, as provided for in the agreement concluded between the department of criminology and the CDC.

The pre-experimental phase of the CDC took place from October 24, 1972 to June 8, 1973. On May 14, 1973, however, yet another escape took place. Jean-Paul Mercier, Michel Lafleur, Gilles Gingras, Robert Imbeault and André Ouellet, by taking to the fields, sounded the death knell for that centre of destruction, "Laval Ultra-Max." At least, temporarily. The remaining prisoners were transferred and, for a while, Director Goulem, psychologists Williams and Thiffault and the secretary were the only people there.

A Mr. Finstein from the Parliamentary Library prepared a report on the institution. It detailed a number of serious shortcomings, notably the all-pervasive lack of supervision of personnel, the inadequacies of the CDC administration and the lack of communication between the functionaries and the correctional officers.

Director Goulem was subsequently demoted on the grounds of incompetence but, after certain representations had been made, was returned to his functions in March, 1974. He stuck adamantly to his argument that the guards had deliberately allowed the inmates to escape so as to sabotage his "progressive" programmes. This martyr's version of the event still lingers in inside circles, given a new boost by Goulem's remark, during his testimony to the sub-committee, that he feared certain guards more than he did the prisoners. However, a bit of research into his directives within the institution and his numerous reports to Ottawa demonstrate that the horrors which succeeded each other for years at the Special Correctional Unit had all taken place on his orders. There is no doubt that he is defending his own personal views on the system of imprisonment. However, opportunism can always find another path, and the proposed measures in fact cause a much more absolute form of totalitarianism than does the random act of brutality by a guard, since their intention is to use scientific techniques to brainwash the prisoners.

The Correctional Development Centre (still known by the initials SCU) was to continue to hit the headlines. In April 1974, the buildings, on the orders of Commissioner Faguy, were modified so as to house pre-liberation prisoners — those who were soon to be set free and had permission to work outside, returning each night to the SCU. Then came another turn of the wheel: now the CDC was to hold psychiatric patients. This brought on a new wave of construction and modification which has timidly continued from October 1973 to the present day: common rooms, observation posts, kitchen, gymnasium, all were added to the existing cement monster. The authorities are obviously awaiting an opportune moment to reopen the institution. The September 1976 revolt at Laval provided the ideal "emergency" pretext.

Some sixty prisoners were incarcerated in the gas chambers. Their number rapidly grew to one hundred, for an equal number of guards.

The horror began again. In the following weeks, there were gassings and brutality, isolation punishment, six attempted suicides — public attention increased with each new incident.

A secret meeting in December 1976 discussed the future orientation of the institution. The old team rose from its ashes. Messrs. Goulem (still director of the Marineau institution, responsible for regional security) and Jourdain (also responsible for programmes at the regional centre) drew up "an operational plan for the programme for 'Dangerous Inmates' (region of Québec)." The committee was called a "joint" one because, for form's sake, three representatives of the guards' union had been included: Messrs. Gagné, Chalut and Bernatchez. Why include them? Simply because those men (despite their illusions to the contrary) have no power other than to endorse decisions made by the authorities. The administrators wanted their "collaboration" because they would make marvellous scapegoats when the inherent brutalities of the programme reappeared.

And now for the "new" CDC programme:

Under the heading of criteria for the selection of prisoners, it was settled that "the deciding factor for admitting an inmate to the programme would be evidence of his high potential for posing a danger to personnel."[100]

It was noted that "past actions, whether in an institution or on the outside, must be analyzed and used in the process of establishing the potential danger posed to personnel."[101]

Some indicators were then listed: prisoners sentenced to life for first-degree murder; prisoners who had already

156

used physical violence against prison personnel; prisoners who had a history of taking the law into their own hands, especially against peace officers; prisoners whose behaviour toward others or personnel indicated a heightened possibility of future violence against personnel; prisoners convicted of rape, kidnapping, hostage-taking or sequestration.

There were three main elements to the programme: the cell, workshops for non-productive work (basket-making, macramé, etc.) and sports. In order to be eligible for transfer, the prisoner, upon psychiatric evaluation, had to meet the following criteria:

"a) lack of hostility and presence of a positive attitude toward fellow inmates and personnel;

b) favourable evaluation by professional personnel as to degree of dangerosity; and

c) demonstration of successful adaptation to the personnel and to the normal population of the institution."[102]

But it seems it was still extremely difficult to get the new programme under way — not because of humanitarian objections, but because of internal power struggles.

And so we had the solicitor-general announcing that it would be a straight ultra-maximum security institution, while other "experts" (like regional director Le Corre) were arguing against this continued orientation.[103]

It is entirely logical that "graduates in repression" would be attracted to such "fascinating" experimental work in the field of destruction. After all, what is the value of theories and techniques that hardly ever receive any application? And when you are dealing with dangerous prisoners, surely no holds are barred?

The Refinement of Techniques

"Prison may function as a training centre for academics, notably for students of medical psychiatry, pedagogy, social work, psychology, law, sociology, theology, architecture and nutrition."

Goulem Report, p. 349

The special corrections unit is an excellent example of an institution where behaviour-modification programmes are being applied systematically and without reservation. And even if the experiments here have suffered certain setbacks, one must not think that similar procedures have not been experimented with elsewhere. They have—and much more than the public may think. The catalyst was the abolition of the death penalty. Thereafter, it was full steam ahead, for the apparatus of repression urgently needed to find replacements for the solution which had been eliminated.

The self-styled very liberal (in the non-partisan sense of the word) Warren Allmand gave a speech to this effect which—mysteriously—received little publicity. It took place at the February 27, 1976 meeting of the Canadian Club, in the presence of the chairman of the Law Reform Commission, Judge Lamer, and some twenty representatives of the Council of Churches committee for justice and criminology.

Mr. Allmand declared "that he was interested in a whole range of measures designed to modify inmate criminal behaviour, such as the medically-supervised use of drugs and other pharmaceutical products, psycho-surgery, and other methods which lay somewhere between capital punishment and life imprisonment for murder."[104]

Let us now examine some of these aberrations which are being used in both Canada and the United States against prisoner/guinea pigs, stripped of all their rights.

Control By Medication

In Canadian prisons, medications—chemical strait jackets—are widely used to control the captives. Federal Member of Parliament Leggett, a member of the sub-committee on penitentiaries, asked J. W. Braithwaite, deputy commissioner of programmes:

> "... in the list I have of drugs dispensed in various institutions, Joyceville has an incredible amount of drugs that are being dispensed. Are we drugging these people to get them into work programmes or what is going on? You are looking at 306,786

instances of drugs being administered in Joyceville with a population of 450."

Leggett later added:

"I am sure they are accurate in reporting, say, psychotropic drugs... They would surely know how many psychotropic drugs were administered and I think it leads the country... There are 24,326 psychotropic drugs administered at Joyceville... Why does Joyceville administer that many psychotropic drugs."[105]

And Mr. Craigen—who, incidentally, is director-general of medical services (!) for the Canadian Penitentiary Service—offered this definition of what the term includes:

"A psychotropic drug covers... a vast range of drugs, ranging from such things as valium tranquilizers through Largactil, which might or might not be used for schizophrenia, to amine oxidize inhibitors which would be used for endogenous depression. Essentially, it is almost any drug that has an effect on the mind, on the psyche."[106]

When questioned about the products being used at Penetanguishene (a provincial institution in Ontario), which Member of Parliament Leggett termed "one of the most outstanding institutions in the country."[107] the director-general replied:

"Basically, my impression is that you have some basic therapeutic programmes plus the use of new medical techniques and then things like the very controlled use of LSD in certain situations."[108]

Repression by medication is much more practical for the authorities, especially since the title of "treatment" justifies all abuses.

It is therefore irrelevant to dwell on abuses in psychiatric institutes in the USSR, a phenomenon which the bourgeois press loves to cover in detail, since the same kind of torture exists in Canadian penal institutions. It is more important to know the basic history, use and consequences of these chemical products. An article in *L'Express*, under the name of Pierre Accoce, gives us some interesting details.[109]

Psychiatric chemistry was born in France. As early as 1952, its possibilities were being explored by Professors Jean Delay and Pierre Deniker. At the time there was only one neuroleptic (or psychotrop) on the market, chlorpromazine, better known under the brand name of Largactil. Now there are more than twenty, all derived from two family groups, the butyrophenomes and the phenothiazines, and in world-wide use.

Without exception, these drugs induce a state of passivity. They are used in order to mitigate crisis or chronic psychosis, and they reduce agitation and aggression.

Some act more directly on the nervous system than others, and may even cause hallucinations (especially haloperidol), but all these products end up causing generally passive behaviour. The neuroleptics act on the central nervous system. They diminish the secretion of substances by the hypothalamus and the pituitary which regulate the production of hormones and so regulate the life of the organism. The medications effectively "jam" the reflexes, though they do not anaesthetize them or induce sleep. While they do not alleviate any specific problem, they do — by setting in motion a neurological process which is not yet understood — reduce swings of mood associated with severe psychotic disturbances.

In short, the side-effects may be more serious than the original problems. Some argue that these neuroleptics are, literally, cerebral poisons that attack the personality, but other pharmacologists (who, no doubt, have monetary interests at stake) claim that they are the least toxic of all medications. Whichever may be the case, their side effects are disturbing: loss of weight, dryness of the mouth, constipation, retention of urine, impotence in men and frigidity in women, sensitivity to light, and tremors that resemble those of victims of Parkinson's disease.

After 1957, undoubtedly because of efforts being made to eliminate these side-effects, a new class of drugs has emerged derived from imipromine: anti-depressants. Initially tested by a Swiss doctor, Professor Roland Kuhn, then by Professors Delay and Deniker, they were not very quickly brought into use. As their name indicates, they are specifically designed to counter depression. Patients treated with these drugs swing beyond euphoria to manic excitement. Under the influence of these drugs, depressives who are latent suicide candidates often make an actual suicide attempt. To eliminate this risk, neuroleptics are administered as well, so as to numb their minds. Like the neuroleptics and, again, without anyone quite knowing why, the anti-depressants act on the central nervous system and the reflexes. Their side-effects include: accelerated heartbeat, hypertension, problems in focusing with attendant difficulties in reading and conceptualizing. Often, the prisoners, knowing that these products are available, request them, because they want to forget their surroundings.

And so, the Canadian Penitentiary Service is able to reduce the number of prison revolts, destroy physically and psychologically those who are under its power and, finally, experiment with behaviour modification and other techniques.

Brainwashing, Shock Treatments, etc...

"I believe that Dr. Workman subjected inmates to brainwashing; he demoralized them so he could more easily mould them afterwards." Member of Parliament Robinson during one of the hearings of the sub-committee.

Brainwashing programmes are not just the stuff of science fiction and "B" movies. Every penitentiary, to a greater or lesser degree, in a more or less acknowledged fashion, tries to modify surreptitiously the behaviour and the values of the prisoners. The attempts are unremitting: the physical structure of a detention centre lends itself beautifully to the endeavour and, for many prisoners, the universe consists of a cell, 23 hours and even 24 hours a day. Despite appearances, the chaplain and the psychologist are faithful accomplices of the armed guard.

All scientific techniques for behaviour modification are based on the work of the American psychologist Skinner, whose studies may be summarized under the formula: reward/punishment. It was another American psychologist,

Edgar H. Schein, who systematized this theory for brainwashing purposes.[110]

Taking as his groundwork the experiments which had been carried out on American war prisoners during the Korean war in the early Fifties, Schein devised an infallible technique for the transformation of individuals. The method is based on a dual principle.

First, says Schein, in order to bring about profound modification of behaviour and/or attitudes, it is necessary to weaken, undermine, or remove the supports to the old patterns of behaviour and the old attitudes.

Second, the person carrying out the programme must have total control over the environment of the person being treated — that is, there must be complete isolation from the outside world. Obviously, penitentiaries in general and institutions such as the special correctional unit in particular meet this condition perfectly. And then treatment begins. The break with the outside world is not enough. The patient must also be isolated within the treatment environment, in order to prevent the development of group solidarity and an attendant sub-culture. Natural leaders, therefore, those with the ability to influence the group as a whole, are segregated, and every possible means is employed to sow suspicion and discord among group members.

Those running the programme then make constant calls for the prisoners' co-operation and voluntary participation. Having been cut off from their customary behaviour models, the prisoners' suggestibility is greatly increased — especially, of course, if the psychologists and other leaders, professionals who exude authority, manage to win their confidence.

Another stage: the prisoner or prisoners are placed in a situation where they must rise to a challenge in order to win the approval of the authorities.

The objective may be to modify one character trait or to change behaviour entirely.

Finally, constant pressure, based on the reward/punishment system, leads the subject toward the desired attitudinal changes. Prisoners who have already been through the programme may very effectively be used to indoctrinate others in turn.

With most subjects, brainwashing is accomplished in a matter of months.

Though Schein largely devoted himself to the theoretical side of the process, other psychologists, James V. McConnell in particular, worked on the applications which might be made of the theory for the treatment of criminals[111]. This specialist in experimental psychology, for whom a rat in the laboratory or a prisoner in a penitentiary were to be treated in the same reward/punishment way, had no compunctions about using brainwashing techniques on those whom the legal system failed to subdue. He was interested in combining brainwashing with sensory deprivation (that is, absolute control of the environment) for more effective treatment. It was at about this same time during the Fifties that Dr. Hebb, psychology professor at McGill University, carried out his studies on the relationship between perception and the environment.

At the height of the Cold War, the Canadian government noticed that the military personnel running the DEW line installations in the Arctic Circle, who lived in complete isolation, proved to be vulnerable to the propaganda programmes on Radio Moscow. Hebb suspected that it was the impoverishment of the environment, the lack of stimuli, which had made these men so suggestible.

But he had no proof. And so he ran experiments with student subjects, paying them $20 a day (which was a lot, at the time) to do nothing, while confined in an isolation chamber, deprived of sound and visual perceptions, lying stretched out on the bed, being fed and sheltered. The experiment, which was to last six weeks, had to be dropped after a few days because of the severity of the disorders—such as hallucinations and mental deterioration—which appeared. Professor Hebb himself summarized the dangers of such a régime, which is present to some degree in every penitentiary, when he spoke before the sub-committee:

> "The experimental evidence is quite definite. The complete isolation for a period of three days or

more has a demonstrable effect on the deterioration of the functioning of the brain, disintegration of the personality — in effect, a process of destruction of personality and mind. The evidence that we have consists of studies of isolation up to a period of six days, which was as long as any student could stand it. And we were paying them handsomely; paying them at the rate of a professor at the time, and they were hard up in wanting to earn as much money as possible. Few could last more than three days. The longest anyone stood was six days. At the end of that time there was a recovery that took four or five days. The effects of longer periods I cannot do more than make an educated guess at, but it is clear that the effect was a steady deterioration of the personality, a genuine destructive process. In our experiments, continued as long as they were, there was, as far as we know, complete recovery. But there is always danger that those students of ours who could only last one day might have had a permanent change of their thoughts, and so on, if they had stayed longer."[112]

We thus understand the importance attached by psychologists like McConnell, of course, but also by Thiffault and Co., to the physical structure of the isolation chamber in which their brainwashing is to be carried out. They all echoed the same theme: let us do within the institution that which seems best to us. You handle security about the penitentiary boundaries; leave us free rein inside. Above all, there must be no people unconnected with the experiment allowed to come in and disturb our work. "We are the specialists...," they kept saying. If the Canadian Penitentiary Service has not followed this approach to the letter, if differences arise between, say, Goulem and Le Corre, it is certainly not because of the threat posed to humanitarian principles.

No: above all, it is because the enormous bureaucratic structure of the Canadian Penitentiary Service hesitates to give such freedom of action to groups of professionals without retaining overall control. The professionals, of course, do not wish to accept that residual control. The brainwashing techniques are not only being used in isolated cases like the experiments in the CDC and the programmes carried out at the "residential unit" level and in group therapy; they have also had a systematic application in a pilot project carried on outside penitentiary walls. We are here referring to the "Carrefour Nouveau Monde"* project of Dr. Déom. The project, obviously, has the close co-operation of both the office of the solicitor-general and the CPS. Hand-picked prisoners, especially ones convicted of sexual offences, are subjected to the kind of treatment preached by McConnell. The government provides the project with subsidies — generous ones, it must be added. Under the pretext of social reintegration, psychologist Déom and his team have, since 1973, been carrying out behaviour modification experiments in the Rotage district. The subject's every gesture is watched, and the whole gamut of techniques — financial rewards, prisoner co-operation, spying by video camera, group pressure through "truth sessions" — is used in order to manipulate the patient and destroy him.[113]

Other equally bizarre techniques are being used in penal institutions across the country. Some even seem to resurrect old Nazi dreams. Let us examine what goes on in the Centre for Mental Hygiene in Penetanguishene, Ontario, whose director, Boyd, so favourably impressed the sub-committee during his testimony. One of the specialties of this institution is the treatment of sexual offenders.

Dr. B.A. Boyd:

> "We have a Ph. D. psychologist and a bunch of dirty pictures and a peter meter that you put on the penis and it waves every time something happens. They have a little box that gives an electric shock and the patient gives informed consent. He sets the rate of pain and it is all voluntary. We have a fair number of pedophiles in particular going through that process... [This kind of treatment] should be available somewhere in the federal penitentiary system."[114]

---

* Crossroads of the New World — translator's note.

Having given us this taste of the methods employed in the institution, Dr. Boyd then describes other procedures for the awed members of the sub-committee ("I must say I have never really got over that, it seemed to me the one hope of some form of treatment," declared Member of Parliament Simma Holt[115]).

> "We get signed informed consent for electroshock, any procedure that is going to render him unconscious, like a sodium amytal interview might, any procedure that is painful, like aversion therapy, anything that is a serious invasion of privacy, like our capsule encounter group, where they go in nude and they sort of have to expose themselves psychologically as well."[116]

As well, there are the lobotomies performed at the Philippe-Pinel provincial institution on "mentally ill" prisoners who have been sent there by the Canadian Penitentiary Service. This type of operation was invented by a Portuguese neurologist, Dr. Moniz (1874-1955) and began to be applied in 1935. It consists of a surgical operation to sever connections between nerve cells within the frontal lobe of the brain. The goal is to transform particularly violent and obsessive individuals into inoffensive vegetables.

The procedure (which has been condemned in the USSR) enjoys great favour on the part of certain particularly repressive psychiatrists, and constitutes the system's ultimate weapon — apart from the death penalty — for the definitive neutralization of its marginal members.

And to think that the MacGuigan report mentioned with horror such practices as "a 'cure' for mental defectives, plunging in a trough of ice and slush (abolished in the 1930s)."[117]

Finally, to conclude our discussion on shock tactics, there are all the experiments being tried on prisoners which seem to cause no embarrassment to anyone at all.

Michael Mills and Norval Morris, in a paper entitled "Prisoners and Laboratory Animals," list the many precedents along these lines in the United States. There were the anti-malarial drugs tested on penitentiary prisoners at Statesville in Illinois, for example, and the new antibiotics administered to prisoners in Indiana on behalf of a pharmaceutical multi-national. Participating prisoners won certain privileges, like packages of cigarettes, or were paid a wage of $2 a day. Captives of the Alabama prison were subjected to blood-plasma research tests; prisoners of the State Penitentiary of Oregon had certain biopsies performed on their testicles, in the name of research into human reproduction.

And then there are all the creams, cleansers and deodorants which are tried out, in pre-marketing trials, on prison inmates in Indiana, and the research into cholera and respiratory problems being jointly conducted at the State Penitentiary of Texas by the university and the College of Physicians. (In this latter case, the prisoners received $5 a day for their service as guinea pigs.) And there were the captives of the State Penitentiary of Vermont, who took part "volun-tarily" in experiments into obesity and diabetes, under the kindly eye of the director of the institution. And all these horrors take place, despite the statements of the Helsinki Declaration on treatment of prisoners, and despite the world-wide reaction of the medical fraternity to the monstrous Nazi experiments along these same lines.

In Canada, this situation receives little publicity. The only experiments of which we have heard involved various brands of shampoo and cigarettes and took place at the Leclerc Institute, part of the Laval Penitentiary complex. Sometimes, though, tiny items at the bottom of the newspaper page (like the one below) give us an idea of what is going on in the penitentiaries—though of course nobody reacts to the news, since it is all happening in another country!

Experiments on Prisoners
WASHINGTON—The American Atomic Energy Commission bombarded the testicles of 131 prisoners in Oregon and Washington with X-rays during the 1960s in order to determine if such powerful radiation levels would cause sterility, a spokesman attached to the research and development branch today confirmed.

Another interesting phenomenon: the extension of repression beyond prison walls.

In the universities, the system is seeing to the formation of large numbers of specialists to do surveillance work in the marketplace. To give just one specific example, the Criminology School of the Université de Montréal has, since the early 1960s, trained some 500 specialists for their place in the system. These people are probation officers, whom we don't think of as being part of the penitentiary, but who nonetheless discreetly supervise the comings and goings of their "clients." They are psychologists, who provide the police force with required personality profiles. They are social workers who administer pre-sentencing examinations that help determine the prisoner's classification upon arrival at the Reception Centre of the CPS. This is a significant and threatening development, since it leads to a great deal of social-science experimentation in the field of techniques of control. Commissioner Therrien told the sub-committee:

> "I believe a researcher from the United States, Martinson, made an assessment of, I think, more than 100 different techniques of readaptation being employed in many parts of the United States and here, with an assessment as to what their efficiency is."[118]

Thus, all the talk being mouthed by the authorities about finding substitutes for imprisonment does not, in the end, promise us a reduction in the number of prisoners inside the institutions, but rather, an increase in the amount of repression outside the institutions. The oppression of the semi-prisoner is so much more economical: $1,500 a year rather than the $15,000 needed for an actual prisoner!

An excellent way to win over public opinion.

Conclusion

Photo Credit: Pierre Gaudard. Prison for Women (Kingston).

The Long Preparation
For Escape

One must clearly understand that before penitentiaries, or any other institutionalized form of torture, can be abolished, the State itself, of whatever type, must first be abolished. At the most fundamental level, therefore, the struggle against prisons is part of the movement to fully radicalize politics. As we have seen, prison isolation grew along with the modern State and developed in response to the repressive needs of the economic system which it supports: capitalism. This is the situation world-wide. It is why we find, everywhere on our planet, that the State and its corollary, the penitentiary, survives in one form or another. Whether in Canada or the United States, in Chile, in the USSR or China, though under many different pretexts (the repression of the criminals and bandits; eliminating terrorists; neutralizing "traitors to the motherland"; elimination of the "bourgeois" that lurks in every person's breast, everywhere), we find that a minority of workers are imprisoned so that the majority of workers may be exploited as a labour force.

The prisoners must never forget, despite the undeniable singularity of their position, that every struggle of the working class is theirs as well.

Therfore—despite all the prejudice in our society against the "criminals," the "cons"—the trade-union fight for better working conditions; women's fight for liberation; the ecological battle to protect the environment; the struggles of the unemployed, those on welfare, ethnic minorities and native peoples... all are part of the same defiance of the same enemy.

But these objective connections do not mean that the prisoners' struggle should be directed by the other protest groups. Absolutely not: prisoners must define their own strategy, with all its particularities, but they should do so without ever forgetting (as the political authorities would so like them to forget) that their fight cannot be separated from that of the working class as a whole.

These larger considerations lead us to elaborate the main elements of a strategy for the abolition of prisons.

First element: *information*

It is extremely important that the population know what is going on behind the penitentiary walls. This book, whatever its limitations, is a response to that challenge. Every effort of this sort must be encouraged. Books by prisoners and ex-prisoners, the testimony of interested parties, families, friends and support groups... in every possible way, we must throw light where the authorities wish darkness to reign. The penitentiary gains much of its power from the silence, the confusion, that surrounds it. Priority must be given, therefore, to providing as much information as possible, so as to disturb the present placid indifference as much as possible.

Second element: *the judicial guerilla*

Prisoners continue to suffer a host of injustices that have long since been condemned in the law books. Since prisoners' immediate well-being is so important, we must take these injustices to the courts. Not a few cases here and there, but *en masse*. It's not good enough to protest the inadequate medical care received by prisoner X: representations must be made on behalf of every prisoner in that same position until, finally, the courts yield and pass the laws that will improve conditions of detention. One noteworthy example of this kind of partial victory was the McCann judgment delivered by Mr. Justice Heald of the federal court in British Columbia in 1975.

Furthermore, prisoners themselves should understand the rudiments of legal procedure so that they can take the initiative themselves. The first step, legal advice, may come from specialists, but the movement as a whole must be the work of those who are directly concerned. In our opinion, that is the true base for genuine liberation.

Third element: *organizing the prisoners*

As in any social struggle, organizing is essential to the combat within prison walls.

The prisoners' committee is the ideal organizing force — on condition, naturally, that it has not been infiltrated (as is too often the case) by a puppet loyal to the authorities.

This committee, democratically elected by the prisoners, wholly controlled by them, must struggle, via a combination of negotiation and pressure tactics, to wrest two things from the authorities: legal recognition for itself (it should have, a constitution) and rights for the prisoners — for all they have at the moment is a number of privileges, which vary with the humour of the administration.

The expression "pressure tactics" may cause a few wrinkled brows. Remember that the preliminary text of the MacGuigan report seemed to approve of peaceful disobedience by prisoners as a means of protest. The MPs even cited the 1976 Archambault strike as an example of what they meant.

The committee, in order to protect its defensive role, must not degenerate into a combined social convenor and mouthpiece for messages from the director. Its function is to express and champion prisoners' grievances, and it must never allow itself to be manoeuvred into filling the inherent gaps in penitentiary systems. As well as carrying out the functions which have already been mentioned, the committee may distribute various tasks among its members; for example, watchdog roles in the areas of grievances, medical care, working conditions, and so on. The committee has an obvious educational role as well: it must take people's individual histories and provide the synthesis; lead projects designed to improve conditions of detention; organize study groups around works dealing with penitentiary issues and the politico-economic social system of society, the history and function of repression, actions undertaken by prisoners' committees in other parts of Canada and throughout the world, etc.

If they have had this kind of training, prisoners, upon regaining their freedom, will be capable of continuing the struggle on the outside, rather than just drowning their memories "in a beer or two with the guys." It is prisoners themselves who will bring about the liberation of prisoners.

Final element: *popular education and mobilization*

As we have already said, the general population must know what is going on inside those walls, what fate is in store for the prisoners.

In a sense, there is plenty of news—whenever something spectacular happens. The bourgeois media report the events faithfully; it's just that they never explain the reasons *why* these things are happening. It is therefore necessary — and this little "workbook" may be of help—to give popular groups a clear explanation of the penitentiary system and its effects. In this way, unions, student circles and citizen committees may more easily grasp the various phenomena associated with criminality, and combat the biases of the sensationalist press.

The prisoners' struggle would then enjoy more widespread outside support and perhaps some day, who knows, a mass movement for the abolition of prisons. Furthermore, popular education about penitentiaries would contribute to the present political debate about the formation of an opposition of the Left. Unfortunately, activists too frequently

174

underestimate the degree of repression that exists in advanced industrialized countries like Canada, and think it's enough to use Third-World case histories to explain the brutality of a régime. Another frequent weakness in the activists' approach is that too many of them depend on theoretical notions like "the dictatorship of the proletariat," while knowing virtually nothing of the repression actually being practised in the country. If they knew more about the mechanisms of the repressive apparatus in the country, they could draw parallels between régimes that are supposedly antithetical to each other, but in fact speak the same language: "rehabilitation of criminals" or "re-education of anti-social elements" comes down to the same thing. Studying the facts would lead them to the conclusion that whenever a worker is imprisoned, in whatever country, it is in order to increase the degree of control being exercised over a thousand others.

Popular education is just as important. It must be aimed at the professional groups whose members, directly or indirectly, participate in the development and maintenance of the repressive policies of the system. It is not surprising that intellectuals, victims of their own training and/or financial interests, are frequently complicit in the injustices being done the prisoners. The journalist who covers the police beat, the lawyer who defends a client, the professionals of the various social sciences, the psychologists, the criminologists, the sociologists, the social workers and doctors... many of them, quite unconsciously, contribute to the repression even as they assume they are helping liberalize the régime.

And a radical perspective, broader than the usual "professional" analysis inculcated into each of these groups, would help. It might not lead to the creation of groups like the GIP in France (Groupe d'Intervention sur les prisons,"* founded in 1971 by Michel Foucault), but at least it would increase the number of people sympathetic to the prisoners' cause.

Social activists should not only provide their audiences with information during these educational campaigns, but

---

* Group for Prison Intervention — translator's note.

ask them questions as well. What do people think about crime? Prisons? Alternatives to prison? The abolition of these institutions? The authorities in charge of criminal and penal matters? Rehabilitation? The true functions of the State and its apparatus for repression? etc...

Increased understanding of crime and of prisoners will contribute to the liberation of all workers.

The struggle for the abolition of prisons is more than a matter of knocking down the walls. As Oscar Wilde said, "Four walls do not a prison make." No, the struggle against the penitentiary is above all the struggle against the social system that creates such an institution. Viewed from that perspective, all prisoners are political prisoners.

Appendices

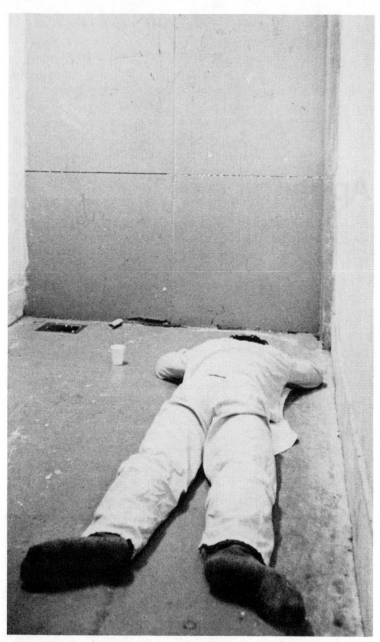

Photo Credit: Pierre Gaudard. Archambault.

1. Presentation of the Archambault Manifesto

The Manifesto printed below should be understood in its historic context, for it marks one of the most bitter struggles ever to erupt in the Canadian penitentiary system. On January 14, 1976, about 350 prisoners of the Archambault maximum-security institution (part of the Ste. Anne des Plaines complex) began a work strike to force an improvement in their living conditions and to express sympathy for the strike already in progress at St. Vincent de Paul.

All through the previous summer and fall, the prisoners had repeatedly asked that conditions in the penitentiary be brought up to the level that any sane society would demand. But nothing happened.

And so the strike marked an important step for the prisoners: written requests gave way to mass action designed to force the authorities to recognize them as a valid partner in a valid dialogue. Two days after the action began, the prisoners' committee contacted the Human Rights League and one of its working committees, the Office for Prisoners' Rights, and asked that it serve as mediator in the conflict. The Office accepted. One week later, the strikers' main demands were made public. Many of them had to do with living conditions in the institution, but the main ones concerned the right to physical contact with their visitors—that is, the right not to be separated from their visitors by a pane of glass. As some of the strikers pointed out, many of them had not embraced their wives or children for years. One claimed to have suffered this deprivation for fifteen years.

They also wanted a lot more information about the mysterious death by cyanide of a prisoner named Laurence.

On February 9, faced with a complete lack of response from the administration, the prisoners' committee drew up a list of six mediators who they wanted to have confront the authorities on their behalf. The six were: Jean-Claude Berheim, of the Office for Prisoners' Rights; Nicole Daigneault, a lawyer known for her activities on behalf of political prisoners; Jean Serge Masse, lawyer; Dr. Serge Mongeau, a militant community activist; Laurent Laplante, journalist; and Robert Burns, a PQ member of the National Assembly and former CSN trade unionist. Suddenly, on February 11, the prison administration gave its first signs of life. Director Lebrun announced he was opposed to the very principle of negotiation, but would nonetheless allow access to Sachitelle (who had acted as mediator during the St. Vincent de Paul conflict). Sachitelle, after reading the whole dossier, commented: "The prisoners have formulated well-structured demands which aim at nothing less than a complete change in the very philosophy of the maximum-security institution."

The journalist, Laplante, was finally also accepted by the Archambault administration and on February 24, almost a month and a half after the strike had started, negotiations began.

Lebrun's about-face had been caused by two things: the prisoners' determination, and the ever-so-slightly liberal policy laid down one year earlier (February 7, 1975) by Commissioner André Therien to the effect that thereafter a given prison administration was to enter into genuine negotiations with representatives elected by prisoners of that institution.

The strike continued, despite horrifying conditions. Meals, reduced to two a day, generally consisted of baloney sandwiches. Sanitary conditions were disgusting, and the men

180

were confined almost permanently to their cells.

But striker solidarity held firm. Outside support grew as the conflict dragged on.

As soon as the strike began, the wives, families and friends of the prisoners organized a support group, the "Organization de soutien de la lutte des prisonniers (OSLP)."* The group publicly supported the strikers' demands and staged two demonstrations, one in front of St. Vincent de Paul and Archambault (on February 2) and the other in front of the Montréal office of the federal solicitor-general and the home of Director Lebrun (on February 15).

Québec personalities and prison-support groups joined in. André Normandeau, director of the department of criminology at the Université de Montréal, was one: he wrote an open letter which pointed out that the main point of contention, the right to physical contact during visits, had been accepted 15 years earlier in the maximum-security institutions of Sweden, Norway, Denmark, Finland and Holland, and had presented no difficulties whatsoever. Warren Allmand, however, replied that "it would be impossible to permit" such visits. On April 22, the John Howard Society publicly asked Solicitor General Allmand to take personal charge of the Archambault situation.

Prisoners and former prisoners saw how important it was to support the Archambault action. On February 10, the prisoners of the provincial Bordeaux prison began a sympathy hunger strike (which was quickly suppressed). Two former St. Vincent de Paul prisoners, Gilbert Groleau and Richard Bertrand, blew themselves up along with the bomb they were trying to place in a bus station as a gesture of support for the strike. Their choice of a would-be target, however, gave the authorities the perfect pretext for an anti-prisoner publicity campaign (conducted at the usual fever pitch of hysteria).

As in any other strike situation, the authorities responded violently.

On January 27, Louis Henry, vice-president of the prisoners' committee, was beaten by an anti-strike goon. As

---

* Support Organization for the Prisoners' Fight—translator's note.

salve for his wounds (and its own conscience) the administration benevolently arranged a private film-screening for him in the prison gymnasium.

Let it be added that the brawl took place under the amused eyes of five guards.

Then, on February 28, another prisoner, André Tessier, was beaten, gassed and finally thrown in the "hole" by three guards. His offence, according to their justification for their behaviour, was that he had illegally cleaned his cell...

Judge Morand, when he received a grievance a few weeks later about this incident, rejected Tessier's allegations out of hand. "The Court," said this judicial bureaucrat, "is of the opinion that grounds have not been established for a warrant to be issued against those involved in the alleged incident and, moreover, guards have full authority to decree isolation for a prisoner." These words of wisdom were to have their effect.

On April 14, Louis Henry was once again beaten by the prisoner in the pay of the authorities, and hospitalized.

Seven days later, Conrad Bouchard and Richard Riddez were wounded by a .12 bullet from the gun of a nervous guard on the other side of the bars.

The Lebrun administration, however, did not lose its composure over such "peccadillos," and called a press conference to assure one and all that the incident had been of no importance.

Despite everything, the prisoners carried on.

On March 10, a few of the demands were accepted, which gave the strikers new heart.

Then, on March 24, negotiations broke down.

They re-opened after a March 31 meeting between the two mediators and Commissioner Therrien.

Mediator Laplante described the atmosphere that reigned at the negotiating table: "The local administration talks constantly of federal directives which make it impossible to reach agreement on the remaining points at issue."

By April 7, matters were deadlocked. But the strike continued.

From then on, the atmosphere was extremely tense. Penitentiary staff, manipulated by the authorities, threatened to launch their own strike if "order isn't soon restored."

The very real possibility of a bloody repression hung over Archambault. And it was in this context that the strikers for the first time became violent themselves. It happened on May 4.

Michel English and Léopold Mercier jumped two guards and threatened to kill them if the authorities did not meet two demands. The two demands were that they be transferred to Workworth, a medium-security institution in Ontario, and that Tessier be removed from isolation (by then he had been in the "hole" for nine weeks).

The suspense continued for 14 hours. The situation was saved by the intervention of William MacAllister, president of the prisoners' committee. The authorities promised the desired transfer.

And the prisoners were indeed sent to Workworth... but for a very short period of time. They were quickly sent on, first to Kingston and then to Millhaven, both of them maximum-security institutions. And Michel English, among others, spent months in isolation.

On May 6, the prisoners ended their strike.

The issue of physical contact during visits had not been settled, but the prisoners had obtained recognition for their committee. Permission was also given for frequent visits to the institution by a citizens' committee.

There were other improvements granted as well, which gave enormous satisfaction to the men who had so courageously resisted for so long, with only their own determination to see them through.

In the summer of 1976, Commissioner Therrien announced that physical contact would be permitted during visits as of March 1977.

And so the action of "the Archambault guys" resulted in an important gain for all prisoners.

On August 10, 1976, a hunger strike was held in every maximum-security institution in Canada, to force the authorities to put an end to the use of isolation as a disciplinary measure. On September 24, a peaceful demonstration in St. Vincent de Paul turned into a riot. Simultaneously, the same thing (plus a hostage-taking) took place in New Westminster, British Columbia. On October 6, it was the turn of Millhaven prisoners to rise up against the barbarous régime.

You know what happened next. The MacGuigan parliamentary committee began its publicized trip across the country to find out what was amiss in Canadian penitentiaries.

The strike by "the Archambault guys" had proved one thing: that the unity and solidarity of a handful of prisoners could overcome the institutionalized brutality of the 10,000 bureaucrats of the Canadian Penitentiary Service!

2. The Just and Legitimate Demands of the Archambault Guys (21 February 1976)

The Archambault guys demand

1. Recognition of the right to a normal sexual life

The exercise of a normal (heterosexual) sex life is *an elementary and fundamental need* for any human being, just like the need for food, physical exercise, etc...

Any constraint, restriction, limitation of this need and the possibilities for satisfying it, can only have serious consequences for the entire emotional, affective and psychological life of the human being concerned.

For us, it cannot be simply a "privilege" to be granted (or withheld) according to the humour of the moment, a gift wrapped up for "temporary absence, code 26" and offered to a guy after several years of imprisonment and only then if he is submissive, but a *right* which must be inalienable, untouchable, as is the right to reasonable and satisfying food, a *necessity* on both the physical and psychological level.

And end the hypocrisy of saying that such a right does not exist, that we exaggerate, that it is not an important human need, that any "normal" *(sic)* person can easily do without it, that you cannot recognize or accept such a thing, here, in prison, for in fact you do recognize it every single day.

Every day you recognize in practice, and you accept by allowing it to happen, the necessity of a certain sexual practice (though even if you opposed it, it would go on just the same).

Every day you "encourage" (by leaving us no other choice), consciously and deliberately, homosexual practices, and you do so with a laugh, a smirk... "They're animals, they're sick..." (says the guards' scab-union)... "Bah! that's normal for them, it's all the same for them..." "They're the same on the outside..." And you're all in favour of it, really — it prevents "problems," it "calms the guys down," it "breaks the tension." You never disturb the "couples"... unless they get really obvious about it.

Guys screwing guys? Oh... that's okay, it's normal... y'know, they're in prison...

But when we ask to have and to live a heterosexual relationship, a normal relationship, to be able to "make" love and live with the women we love who love us... Boy, what a bunch of perverts! It's abnormal! Impossible!

Well, we've had it! we're fed up! we've had all the hypocrisy we can take about "staying in the community" and we've had enough of screwing other guys!

The Archambault guys demand:

A. That their right to a normal and healthy sexual life be recognized.

B. That the logistics necessary to permit the right to a normal sexual life be arranged by management after consultation with the prisoners and their loved ones (wives, girlfriends, mistresses).

2. Visits and Correspondence

The present situation in Archambault as far as visits are concerned can only be described as "disgusting and inhuman." There is no possibility of making any physical contact, not even finger-tips. Panes of glass separate the prisoners from their families, their wives, their children. The number of visits, like the number of visitors, is limited. All conversations are monitored, which makes even a semblance of intimacy impossible. Same thing with the mail. *We won't accept this any longer!*

And don't start talking about security! Since all visitors have to file by an electronic detector before being allowed into the visiting room, the present situation in that room is completely unjustifiable (unless in the name of security stupidity).

The Archambault guys demand:

A. An *immediate* end to the present policy about visits and its replacement by a policy permitting physical contact, which would allow prisoners to establish more human relationships with their loved ones (wives, children, family) and to maintain effective and more human ties with them.

B. Abolition of the limit of five (5) visits per month. No weekly limits.

C. Abolition of all restrictions on the number of visitors allowed on the "visitors' list."

D. That group visits (with families, wives and children) be authorized (at Christmas, Easter, etc...) and held in the gymnasium or, in summertime, in the yard.

E. That the "summer vacation" (15 days) be primarily a chance for prisoners, families, wives and children to get together, rather than a chance for "voyeurs" to make their little "tour of inspection." For three years now, hundreds of men, women and children having filled the courtyard the entire day... why not *our* children? The whole vacation programme of activities should be restructured toward this purpose.

F. That the "private" interview rooms which are available throughout the week to prisoners who wish to meet with their lawyers should be available on Saturdays and Sunday afternoons.

As for correspondence,

The Archambault guys demand:

G. An end to mail censorship (which now prohibits any criticism of the penitentiary system or its administration, etc...)
H. Restoration of correspondence between all the prisoners, male and female, of all the prisons and penitentiaries.
I. Access to all magazines/reviews which meet provincial and federal censorship standards, including magazines put out by prisoners and prison-rights groups (for example, *Tramplin* and *Transmition*).
J. Free distribution of envelopes, stamps and paper (in light of the tiny "salary" we receive...).

3. Socio-cultural Activities

The present situation can very quickly be described, the activities come down to skin-flicks (hey! it's normal, does the guys good... yuh like that, eh?) or Good-Cop-U.S.A. movies (for "rehabilitation"!), and a few discussion groups — very limited and always held in the teeth of the administration's opposition (unless it's a completely irrelevant group, like the one run by the Catholic chaplain).

The repression is such that the two bureaucrats presently responsible for "S.C." have given up even trying to run evening activities at all, because of the obstacles and "restrictions" put in their path.

That is our reality!

For the Archambault guys, socio-cultural activities are one of the few ways of keeping "live" contact with the "changing" reality of the world outside, of keeping ourselves socially alive, and for these reasons the socio-cultural activities must always and in as many ways as possible maintain this contact with outside reality.

The SCAs are the means for the "outside world" to enter the prison, to allow the guys to be aware of the many aspects of life, and therefore...

The Archambault guys demand:

A. The nomination of a prisoner to be responsible for the SCAs (re: the proposal submitted by the Committee last December, see appendix to this manifesto).

B. The establishment of an SCA programme for the whole of the penitentiary population, and in accordance with the orientation that we establish.

C. More time (especially in the evenings) for the various SCA groups.

D. The increase in the number of visitors permitted a group from 25 to 35.

E. Increase in the number of groups. Two can meet in the day and two in the evening, in the Catholic and Protestant chapels, so as to allow every member of the population access to the socio-cultural activity of his choice.

4. Formation of a Citizens' Committee

The "problem" with prisons, the "problem" in Archambault, is the arbitrary nature of the power exercised here, which prefers to operate in complete obscurity, which can do almost anything it likes because "nobody will know," and "nothing will get out," everything will stay inside, buried by the administrative structure.

Prison... Archambault... is a world where petty little tin gods "reign," whose only power is the power granted them by the cover of darkness. In daylight, they would be nothing.

There will not be, there cannot be, any "change," any reform, any humanization, in any degree, until the light of outside society penetrates the prison walls, until the "ordinary world" is involved with prisons.

Given this necessity to open the prison to the outside world, to bring into it the outside population, with *the right to look, to criticize, to make decisions,*

The Archambault guys demand:

A. Immediate formation of a Citizens' Committee with the right to go wherever they choose and with decision-making powers over the administration and prison life.

B. Composition of the Citizens' Committee as follows:
   1) representatives from organized groups (unions, citizens' committees, various associations),
   2) representatives from groups already working with prisoners,
   3) various representatives, etc... etc...

We wish to point out that this proposal was presented on November 3, 1975, and that it was verbally discussed 6 months later. The administration (J.P. Lebrun) at that time verbally accepted it. And that was the last we heard of it...

5. A Constitution and a Prisoners' Committee

A. **The Archambault guys demand** that their constitution (drawn up by them and defining the rights and powers of the prisoners' committee) be accepted as is, in its present state.
   This constitution is similar to the one accepted and approved by the federal administration in the Cowansville prison.

B. That permament, continual means of communication be established between the representatives of the Archambault guys and the members of the citizens' committee. (Telephone calls and sealed letters must be permitted.)

C. That meetings between members of the prisoners' committee (in conjunction with those of the citizens' committee) be held with new guards during their "training programme" *(sic)*.

D. That there be a meeting between the prisoners' committee and new prisoners upon their arrival in the prison.

E. That facilities be provided (technical and financial) for writing, producing and editing a paper, which is to be distributed to all the Archambault prisoners, to other penitentiaries, and to all outside persons or groups which request it. The paper, to be produced by the prisoners, is to be free of all censorship by the staff of any prison.

6. Isolation and the "Hole"

On October 19, 1975. Marcel Lawrence died while locked up in an "isolation" cell.

Suicide? No! It's too easy to dismiss things with this fine "juridical pretext," which explains nothing and hides much... which says nothing but allows all those "imprisoned prison bureaucrats" to have a clear (oh, so clear) conscience...

"C'mon, wasn't us who killed him..." (as the administration put it, when the guys asked for an explanation).

Marcel Lawrence is dead and we're talking about *murder*, a murder for which some people are more directly responsible than others, more directly involved, but of which no one is innocent, for *you know* what isolation means, in a cement box:

ARCHAMBAULT INSTITUTION File: 62(341)
February 16, 1976
To all prisoners:
2. "The present *isolation* (in a cell, surrounded by all the other guys, with books, with radio —

191

we Committee members are adding this remark) is *difficult for all,* and especially for
certain prisoners who under these conditions
develop *serious behavioural problems.* The heads
of the psychological *(sic)* services have identified
some prisoners who have presently developed a
great deal of anxiety..." (which can lead to suicide?)

The Archambault guys demand an immediate end to
these repressive and murderous practices, and we reject the
claim that these are "minor issues which are of no concern to
the other inmates" (Lebrun, *La Presse* 6/2/76, page 1). *This is
our business because these are our lives which may be lost in
those cement cages.*

The Archambault guys demand:

A. *The abolition and immediate closure of the segregation wing (2-0)* (And whether you call them
"isolation cells" or "disassociation" cells doesn't
change a thing. It's not the name we want abolished,
not a certain semantic terminology on paper, but
the reality.)

Two (2) deaths, a number of suicide attempts, seem
to us enough evidence for judgment to be passed on
this inhuman punishment technique.

Reference:

1. On December 30, 1975, Mr. Justice Darrel
Heald handed down judgment on "isolation,"
calling it "cruel" and "unusual" treatment, not
in accord with the norms of public decency, and
without any utility, given the existence of alternatives.

2. Senator Earl Hasling, in a petition to the Canadian Penitentiary Service, asked for the immediate abolition of the practice of isolation and
segregation, claiming: "It is certain that the
Court would have reached a similar verdict if
confronted with these policies in all the federal

maximum-security prisons which make use of these degrading punitive measures reflecting the evil face of a society that allows such procedures and living conditions to exist in the prison system. They are at worst, punitive, and at best, vindictive."

B. *The abolition and immediate closure of the "hole,"* to put an end to this barbarous, punitive, inhuman measure which has no justification, "given the existence of alternatives."

C. The transfer of all adolescents to either medium- or minimum security institutions (list of names attached).

D. The explanation of all regulations and directives to every prisoner upon arrival, including a booklet about parole.

E. The end to the use of gas and its derivatives in any federal penitentiary.

F. The end to trivial disciplinary reports on matters which in most cases could be settled on the spot, with the slightest degree of mutual good will or the mediation of a prisoners' representative.

G. Access for all federal prisoners to their files, whether to read them or to receive copies of the institutional, police or pre-sentencing reports.

H. The transfer of Mr. Briceau, correctional officer, to a position in which he would no longer have any direct contact with prisoners. This individual is repeatedly the instigator of numerous and continual provocations against prisoners. Action to be taken immediately.

7. Health

Health is first and foremost a matter of a healthy environment, that is, an environment which permits the full expression and full, free development of our needs and potentialities, both physical and psychological. Health is also a matter of the freedom of the human organism to react to aggression and external constraints, to modify a repressive environment, to fight.

As far as we are concerned, there are no "sickos" in Archambault, there are men whose physical organisms are more vulnerable in varying degrees to the sick environment of this prison. There are no psychiatric cases here; there are men, human beings, with affective and psychological needs like those of all other human beings, who have varying abilities to "endure" the constraints of this unhealthy atmosphere.

Until now, the prison doctor has just been another "screw": he cared for the guys enough the make sure they could do their time. But there has never been any effort to come to terms with the prison itself, the direct cause. It's not enough to make the environment "bearable," to prevent any impulse to revolt, to cover up the worst effects, to destroy the critical spirit. They stuff us with drugs to prevent suicides and self-mutilations, but they never quite manage to prevent them all, for the sickness (i.e., prison) is too... sick.

It was too sick, for example, on October 19 last, when Marcel Lawrence died, killed by the prison.

To talk about health in the prison is to talk about abolishing the prison, but we know that prison is the product of a certain society (and one of its constituent elements), that it can do no more than reflect that society, reproduce it in miniature. So there will be no abolition of the prison until the society that gives rise to it is abolished.

However, we believe that it is possible in the immediate future to take a step toward greater health by granting these demands concerning the right to a normal and healthy sexual life, the right to "real" visits, to greater creative autonomy and greater responsibility (Prisoners' Committee, work, socio-cultural activities, etc...).

Immediately, therefore, **The Archambault guys demand** the following minor improvements:

A. A complete medical examination for any prisoner upon demand.

B. The installation of a bell (or buzzer) in each of the

three "control" towers in the ranges, so that the guard knows immediately when an inmate is signalling him. The present lights are frequently ignored, or broken, and in certain cases this can create a situation of real danger.

C. The assignment of a prisoners' representative to the hospital, so that he may meet the needs of his comrades.

D. "Improvement" (the kindest word we can use!) in the services offered prisoners who need outside medical care. (Some are still awaiting operations which have been scheduled for more than a year...)

E. Abolition of the present "hole-like atmosphere" in the hospital.

F. Free supply of items of personal hygiene, like shampoo and tooth-paste.

8. Education

To us, talking about education means talking about the chance to acquire an intellectual and practical formation that increases understanding and decreases alienation from things, from reality and from life. A step toward a liberated spirit.

We include within this perspective all socio-cultural activities, training programmes in the workshops, etc...

As far as education is concerned, therefore, and immediately,

The Archambault guys demand:

A. The immediate opening of a special class for illiterate prisoners. Other prisoners will run these classes, with a ratio of one prisoner to three prisoner-students.

There is to be no limit imposed on the number of prisoners who may take these courses. Every prisoner who does not know how to read or write must have the opportunity to take part.

B. A CEGEP-level programme is to be made available to francophone prisoners (anglophone prisoners already have a comparable programme through Dawson College).

C. Permission for those prisoners taking the CEGEP or university courses by correspondence to remain, if they wish, in their cells in the afternoon in order to study. This would permit:

1) more space in the school for other prisoners who wish to take courses,

2) intellectual work in the cell,

3) students to take part, in the evenings, in various athletic and socio-cultural activities.

9. Work

At present, in Archambault, there is no "workshop" and there never has been one, despite what the administration says / thinks, despite what is "supposed" by the technical teams in the "shops," despite the programmes now being tried in the pre-employment shop (15 guys a year!). All that stuff is bullshit...

All there is, is some large cells being used as occupational storage rooms, beautifully equipped... not, however, to teach a trade or technical competence, but purely and simply to "pass time," to dull minds. Here, the "need to work" *(sic)* is interpreted as the need to occupy the guys somehow, to make them forget their situation, to keep them from "brooding," the need to catch them up in a routine where they have nothing to say and nothing to think. It's another drug — wanted, planned and administered in order to alienate any critical capacity, any impulse to challenge the system. Then too, it's useful, it helps keep down the "damage," makes the guys forget their situation. And out there, on the outside, it's the punch line for the old gag about rehabilitation in prison.

But, in fact, everything has been planned and organized so as to destroy any capacity for independent analysis.

196

The guys have to learn to obey their boss, to do as they're told (i.e., ask no questions), do the jobs put before them, make no fuss (or else, the "hole"...), bow down like all the good little proletarians to their boss.

The Archambault guys have decided to put a (definitive) end to this servility.

"Work" *(sic)* must no longer be an instrument of punishment (of blackmail) or humiliation, like mopping guards' offices while they sit around on their fat butts and laugh at us. We refuse to be servants, docile and obedient proletarians in training for the marketplace. We don't want to spend our entire sentences patching mailbags, serving you, mopping up...

We don't want to fritter away our years like this anymore, we don't want to be treated like dumb animals. We don't want to pay the price any longer for your cowardice, your contempt, your bureaucratized, hierarchical irrelevance.

The time we "do" in your godforsaken prison is ours, it is *our time*, it is our lives, and we've decided to take possession of our own time, such as it is, and to use it in profitable, human and constructive ways.

And so,

The Archambault guys demand:

A. The immediate abolition of the principle and the fact of the so-called production shops. The shops must be places devoted to proper and adequate training and apprenticeship to a trade.

We therefore demand the immediate closing of the "make-work" shops, the "places to store the extra guys," the punishment shops. For example, "mailbag," "canvas repair," and so on...

B. The immediate organization, within the structure of these shops, of study and training programmes for specific trades, combining practice with theory, and leading to a degree of professional competence and some "outside" recognition.

197

We'll give as an example the workshop programme "Pre-employment/wood" (with room for exactly 7 or 8 prisoners).

C. The participation by prisoners, through their representatives, in the development of this kind of training programme, and the permanent presence of one of their numbers in the programme.

D. Easy transfer from one workshop to another (training centre), thus allowing the prisoner who is no longer interested in one trade to try something else.
No prisoner is to be "forced" to stay in a workshop and do something he hates.

E. The immediate installation of windows in all workshops, thus admitting daylight where, at the moment, it's permanent blackout.

F. As for health and safety:
1) Routine inspection of all workshops;
2) Insurance against job-site accidents.

G. The immediate abolition of the present system of salary by "grade," which is nothing but a means of dividing prisoners against themselves and of blackmailing them.

We demand the same pay for all, equal to double the amount now being paid for grade 4.

10. Outside Activities

The Archambault guys demand:

A. The immediate establishment of simultaneous activities.

We demand that a large common room in each of the three pavilions be put at the disposal of those prisoners who do not wish to take part in any outside recreational activities or any other from of recreational activity.

198

New Scheduling

Monday - Tuesday - Wednesday - Friday:
from 6:30 p.m. to 7:45 p.m.: a *large common room* at the disposal of those who want to watch TV, play cards, talk, etc... This is also to apply every Sunday evening when there are films, as well as other evenings when there are shows.

Example: the Sunday evening film, from approximately 7 p.m. to 9:15. Those who don't wish to watch the film must have other recreational possibilities in the common room, contrary to the present policy, which is for them to stay in their cells. The Archambault prisoners already spend too much time in their cells, which is psychologically to their detriment.

Saturday and Sunday:
1:30 p.m. to 3:45 p.m.... A large common room is to be at the disposal of those prisoners who wish to watch sports events on television, play cards, talk, etc... This would reduce, if not eliminate, the hostility and conflicts which now exist between the prisoners and the prisoners' committee. At present, the prisoners' committee is effectively forced by the administration to decide which single activity is to be available to the entire population.

Thursday:
We particularly want the use of the common room this evening, because of the pilot project for simultaneous activities which was presented on January 13, 1976. This would give the population a choice between watching the film being presented by the Ciné-Club (which usually begins at 6:45 p.m. and ends around 9:45) or taking part in outside activities. Once again, this would eliminate conflicts between prisoners, and would allow a fair and adequate solution to a present problem.

B. Return to cells is to take place at 11:30 p.m., every evening, and those who wish to take a shower may do so from 10:30 p.m. on.

C. Access to the outside courtyard until 10 p.m. (summer schedule), and the TV rooms from 10 p.m. on (the simultaneous-activity principle).

D. That walks now being taken in the small courtyards on weekend (morning and evening) take place in the large yard instead.

E. That outside courtyard activities, spring through fall, start at 5:30 p.m., to take advantage of the longer days.

11. Personal and Miscellaneous

The Archambault guys demand:

A. Immediate abolition of all prohibitions concerning beards and long hair (shoulder-length).

B. The right to wear and to purchase "jeans," as well as other clothes of our own choice.

C. The right to have in our possession, in our cells, a transistor radio, which is to be obtained either by a member of the family on the outside, purchased with our own money, or in any other manner.

D. The replacement, at least once a year, of the prisoners' underclothing.

E. That the obligatory savings fund be without limit, and controlled by the prisoner concerned. He is to be able to make use of this money as his own personal funds.

F. Winter clothing: — distribution of woolen socks
— boots (replacing the old "gougounes" 1900)

G. Provision of an iron and ironing board in each pavilion (industrial quality).

H. Javel water.

I. The right to receive all books and magazines sold "outside."

J. A reduction of the waiting period for the purchase of books and hobby items.

12. Meals and Feeding

The Archambault guys demand:

A. An end to the policy of meals in cells (communal meals).
B. Improvement in the service of the meals.
C. Renewal of the canteen list every three months. Authorization of a glass pot.

13. Parole and Classification

With reference to the institutional programme, transfer dates and the establishment of criteria for the right to parole (re: "Conditions for Classification," document of October 30, 1975, which has received no reply to date):

The Archambault guys demand:

A. That the Parole Board be obliged to provide a written report to every federal prisoner who is refused parole; also to those whose cases are postponed, which would make it possible for them to improve their presentations and therefore their chances during their next appearance before the Board.
B. A maximum delay of thirty (30) days between application and decision, except for those cases which must be submitted to Parliament for approval.
C. The formation of an independent Committee of the Board, to which a prisoner who has been refused parole may appeal if he feels that the refusal was unjustified.
(Reference: "The Commission operates and functions in tyrannical fashion, since it is not required to explain its decisions to anybody, or to give reasons for those decisions, a practice which is

contrary to the principles of a democracy."
M. B. Laskin, chief justice of the Supreme Court of Canada, in a minority opinion recently handed down concerning the Parole Board.)

14. Press Conference

The Archambault guys demand:

That at the end of negotiations, the members of the Committee may hold a press conference with representatives of the information media (papers, radio, TV).

15. Abolition of Disciplinary Measures

The Archambault guys demand:

A. That any disciplinary action taken because of this work stoppage be immediately nullified, including all disciplinary reports made during the work stoppage for insurbordination, or for having placed blankets in the window frames in an attempt to keep out the cold, or for any other reason.
B. That the wages which have been suspended since January 15, 1976 (in accordance with Directive 232 and divisional instruction 1210) be restored, retroactive to January 15, 1976.
C. That there be no loss of grade for any prisoner or any recrimination because of this work stoppage.
D. That the disciplinary measures taken by the administration on 15 January 1976 be nullified.
E. That no prisoner lose his present position or be transferred to another institution for having taken part in this work stoppage.
F. (These demands are essential and must be met before the Archambault guys will consider a return to normal activities.)

16. The "Scabs"

The Archambault guys demand:

That all the scabs who did not take part in the strike be immediately transferred to another prison.

The strike by the Archambault guys has been consistently non-violent (we cannot say as much for the administration...) and we wish that same spirit of non-violence to continue within these WALLS after the strike. It is for this reason that we demand the transfer of the prisoner-scabs to another prison, so as to prevent any possible reprisals by certain prisoners.

Epilogue
Archambault 1982

It is tragically ironic that the English translation of Luc Gosselin's *Prisons in Canada*, originally written in response to the landmark 110-day work-strike for more humane living conditions at Archambault in 1977, should appear in the wake of Canada's bloodiest prison uprising. The deaths of the three Archambault prison guards and two prisoners on July 25, 1982, are bleak affirmations of the fact that there is no solution to the violence of prison life to be found within the walls of the prisons.

The bare outlines of the events of the desperate uprising are generally well-known. The media, with their morbid fascination for the violence of the oppressed, have seen to that. The screaming headlines focussed on the three butchered guards and only alluded in passing to the everyday degradation and humiliation that is the lot of the prisoner.

In the uprisings aftermath this repression was applied with renewed vigour. Cell-to-cell searches became excuses for the ravaging of the prisoners few personal possessions and general brutalization. Any resistance was met by fusillades of tear gas against the caged prisoners. The day after the gassings the air was still acrid enough to sting the eyes of journalists invited to view the wreckage.

Since the uprising the prisoners have been subjected to 23½ hour lock-ups in their cells. Prisoners have been, until recently, illegally denied access to lawyers and visitors. They continue to be denied access to television, newspapers and magazines and their only meals consist of cold sandwiches served in their cells. Prison authorities expect these conditions to continue for at least a few more weeks.

In contrast to the 1977 uprising, which was well-organized and coordinated through a strong prisoner's committee, the 1982 eruption was a spontaneous reaction to the institutionalized violence of life in a maximum security prison. The overcrowding of the Canadian prison system by the "debris" of the current economic crisis has caused endless delays in the transfer of prisoners from maximum to medium security prisons leading to a steadily rising level of tension at Archambault and other prisons. The appalling conditions of confinement and the large proportion of men condemned to the living hell of a 25-year prison term with no possibility of parole was also a major factor in the uprising. With no chance of release before well into the next century the hope of escape is an ever-present obsession. An explosion was inevitable.

Predictably the weeks following the uprising have seen enraged demands from the guards for increased security and the curtailment of "privileges." Confronted by the desperation of men subjected to an already inhuman regime of discipline and punishment their only response is a call for more guards, more guns and more repression.

As always the prisoner's and their legitimate grievances have been ignored. The investigation into the uprising ordered by Solicitor General Robert Kaplan did not feel it necessary to call upon even one prisoner to testify before it. Instead the uprising is being used as an excuse to launch an all-out assault on such hard won rights as conjugal visits and to issue renewed calls for the return of the death penalty.

In 1980 Donald Yeomans, Commissioner of Correctional Services Canada, in reference to violence at Archambault stated that, "Canadian maximum security penitentiaries are the most open in North America, because the prisoners have access to many different places within each institution. Perhaps this freedom is the cause of the violence." In marked contrast, Jean-Claude Bernheim of the Office of Prisoners Rights speaking of the latest violent eruption at Archambault declared: "It isn't security thats lacking in these institutions but human dignity."

The administration's approach to problems in the prions is always more security. From a purely administrative point of view they may be right. But, historical experience stands in direct opposition to administrative expediency. In the worst hell-holes of Hitler's death camps and Stalin's Gulag desperate men and women confronted impossible odds because there was nothing else to do and nothing left to lose.

The search for a solution to prison violence through greater "security" is a dead-end. In the words of Victor Serge's classic novel on imprisonment, *Men In Prison*: "Modern prisons are imperfectible, since they are perfect. There is nothing left but to destroy them."

Stephen Ellams
for Black Rose Books
September, 1982

FOOTNOTES

(1) Remark made by a retired prison guard before the Sub-Committee on the Penitentiary System. *Minutes of the Proceedings and Evidence of the Sub-Committee on the Penitentiary System in Canada* (hereafter: *MPESC*), 27:18.

(2) *MPESC*, 40:7.

(3) *MPESC*, 1:3.

(4) *Report of the Superintendent of Penitentiaries*, W.S. Hughes, 31 March 1927, p. 16, Ottawa.

(5) *MPESC*, 27:33.

(6) *Archambault Royal Commission Report of 1938*, p. 16, Ottawa, 1938.

(7) Ouimet Report, Canadian Committee on Corrections, *Toward Unity: Criminal Justice and Corrections*, Ottawa, 31 March 1969, p. 308.

(8) Ibid., p. 308.

(9) Ibid., p. 311.

(10) Ibid., p. 316.

(11) Ibid., p. 316.

(12) Ibid., Annex, p. 327.

(13) *Surveiller et Punir: Naissance de la prison*, Michel Foucault, Éditions Gallimard, Paris, 1975, pp. 274-275.

(14) *The Fear of Punishment*, Law Reform Commission of Canada, Ezzat Abdel Fattah, Ottawa, 1976, p. 93.

(15) Ibid., p. 93.

(16) *MPESC*, 40:67.

(17) *The Fear of Punishment*, p. 96.

(18) *Report of the Superintendent of Penitentiaries*, p. 104.

(19) *La Presse*, 6 April 1970.

(20) *MPESC*, 24A:89 (Appendix JLA-935).

(21) *MPESC*, 24A:58 (Appendix JLA-934).

(22) *MPESC*, 27:35

(23) Idem

(24) *Les crimes et les châtiments au Canada français du XVIIe au XVe siècle*, Raymond Boyer, Cercle du livre de France, 1966, p. 496.

(25) *La Presse*, 29 August 1975.

(26) *Asiles*, Erving Goffman, Éditions de Minuit, Paris, 1968, p. 41.

(27) Ibid., p. 46.

(28) Ibid., p. 106.

(29) Ibid., p. 106.

(30) Ibid., p. 107.

(31) Ibid., p. 108.

(32) *Le Monde diplomatique, June,* 1974. Article by Fred Mahr, "Isolement total et privation sensoriette—une nouvelle forme de torture pour les prisonniers politiques."

(33) A number of books have helped in the preparation of this brief history of penitentiaries throughout the world, including:
Surveiller et Punir, Michel Foucault, already cited.
"The Correctional System," Paul Takagi, in *Crime and Social Justice,* winter, 1974.
The Watcher and the Watched, Bruno Cormier.
"Fonctions sociales des prisons aux États-Unis," Bettina Aptheker, in *S'ils frappent à l'aube,* Angela Davis, Edit. Gallimard, 1972.
"Prisons. Their Rise and Development," Harry Elmer Barnes, in *The Story of Punishment (1930-1972).*
Les prisons, Jacques Voulet, P.U.F., in the "Que sais-je?" collection.
Le Précis Dalloz sur la criminologie et science pénitentiaire, G. Stefani, G. Levaneur and R. Jambu-Mer in, Paris, 1979.
"Theoretical Considerations of Prison in General," F.E. Emergy, in *Freedom and Justice Within Walls,* London, 1970.
Alcatraz Island Prison, W.D. Johnston, N.W., 1949.
Also a number of standard reference works, such as:
Le Grand Larousse Encyclopédique, Vol. VIII, 1963.
L'Encyclopaedia Universalis, Vol. 12, 1968.
This seems the appropriate place to deplore the lack of any comprehensive study of the history of penitentiaries, especially for the period 1880-1940.

(34) "Kingston Penitentiary: The Early Decades," Sidney Shoom, in *Canadian Journal of Corrections* (later re-named *Canadian Journal of Criminology and Corrections*), 1966.

(35) *Crimes et châtiments au Canada Français au XXe siècle,* Raymond Boyer, Cercle du livre de France, 1966, p. 496.

(36) *Toward Unity: criminal justice and corrections,* Ouimet Report, (Report of the Canadian Committee on Corrections), Ottawa, 1969, p. 323.

(37) *MPESC,* 40:65.

(38) *La Presse,* June 14, 1965.

(39) *MPESC,* 29A:8-9 (Appendix JLA-S43).

(40) *MPESC,* 37:16

(41) *Toward Unity: criminal justice and corrections,* Ouimet Report, Ottawa, March 1969, p. 1.

(42) *MPESC,* 40:7.

(43) *The Role of Federal Corrections in Canada,* report of the Task Force on the Creation of an Integrated Canadian Corrections Service, Solicitor-General of Canada, Ottawa, January 1977, pp. 28 and 40 respectively.

(44) *The Criminal in Canadian Society—A Perspective on Corrections,* Ottawa, 1973, p. 1.

(45) "The Correctional System," by Paul Takagi, in *Crime and Social Justice,* Winter, 1974, p. 83.

(46) *The History of Violence in America: Historical and Comparative Perspectives,* pp. 346-347, Frederick A. Preager, N.Y., 1969.

(47) *The State in Capitalist Society,* Ralph Miliband, Basic Books Inc., Publishers, New York, 1969.

(48) Ibid., p. 25.

(49) Ibid., p. 26.

(50) *MPESC,* 30:72.

(51) *MPESC,* 23:156.

(52) *MPESC,* 25:37.

(53) *The State in Capitalist Society,* p. 5.

(54) *Monopoly Capitalism,* Paul A. Baran and Paul M. Sweezy, Monthly Review Press, New York and London, 1966.

(55) Ibid., p. 25.

(56) Ibid., p. 71.

(57) Ibid., pp. 71-72.

(58) Ibid., p. 9.

(59) *Canada Year Book* (for each year mentioned), Ottawa.

(60) *Monopoly Capitalism,* p. 11.

(61) Ibid., p. 66.

(62) *Annual Report of the Solicitor General* (for each year mentioned). Our information for 1977-78 derives from a provision found in section 16 of the proceedings and evidence of the Standing Committee on Justice and Legal Affairs (26 May 1977) during the presentation of the budget for the Ministry (p. 140 for the cited figures). May we add that, in our experience, it is exceedingly difficult to obtain information and statistics from this Ministry. Despite its personnel, which has risen to 231 people and $12.1 million, we often found it necessary to consult a variety of governmental publications in order to come up with basic information about this Ministry. These gaps, however, are undoubtedly fully justified on grounds of security!

(63) *Canada Year Book* and various other figures from Statistics Canada for the years in question.

(64) *Canada Year Book,* for each year mentioned.

(65) *MPESC*, 40A:82 (Appendix JLA-59).

(66) *Report of the Superintendent of Penitentiaries.*

(67) *La Presse*, 18 February 1970.

(68) *A Manifesto of Criminal Policy*, by Manuel Lopez-Rey y Asseyo, former head of the Crime Prevention and Criminal Treatment Section, General Secretariat of the United Nations.

(69) *MPESC*, 25:14.

(70) For the years 1930-1949, *Annual Report of the Commissioner of Penitentiaries*, 31 March 1949, in which appeared a cumulative table. For the years thereafter, the annual reports and the figures compiled in the *Canada Year Book.*

(71) MPESC, 40:121.

(72) *Annual Report of the Commissioner, Report of the Solicitor General*, and *Canada Year Book* for the cited years.

(73) *MPESC*, 25:26.

(74) *MPESC*, 40:78.

(75) *The State in Capitalist Society*, pp. 52-53.

(76) *Fonction sociale des prisons aux États-Unis*, by Bettina Aptheker, p. 51.

(77) "Les critères de sélection utilisés au Centre de réception de St-Vincent de Paul," unpublished Master's thesis, Claude Gaulin, Université de Montréal, 1972.

(78) *MPESC*, 25:6.

(79) *MPESC*, 40A:82 (Appendix JLA-59).

(80) *MPESC*, 40A:81 (Appendix JLA-59).

(81) *Report of the Sub-Committee on the Penitentiary System in Canada*, May 1977, paragraph 636, p. 148.

(82) Ibid., paragraph 638, p. 132.

(83) *MPESC*, 27:32.

(84) *MPESC*, 21:49.

(85) *MPESC*, 40:129.

(86) *The Criminal in Canadian Society*, p. 17.

(87) Ibid., p. 18.

(88) *MPESC*, 30:25.

(89) *Report of the Task Force on Plans for Maximum-Security Institutions*, Ottawa, 1971, p. 11.

(90) *Report of the Sub-Committee on the Penitentiary System in Canada*, p. 81.

(91) *Psychologie*, Paris, October 1973.

(92) *Soumission à l'autorité*, Stanley Milgrams, Calmann-Levy, 1974.

(93) *Manual of Correctional Standards*, New York, 1966, p. 334.

(94) *La Presse*, 8 December 1965.

(95) Ibid., 31 December 1965.

(96) Ibid., 22 August 1972.

(97) Ibid., 26 August 1972.

(98) Ibid., 20 March 1973.

(99) Testimony from *Indications pour une thérapie de groupe en milieu pénitentiaire*, in the chapter "Phase pré-expérimentale du Centre de développement correctionnel," Volume 11, by the Lagier study group, unpublished, Université de Montréal, 1973.

(100) "Proposition de plan d'opération pour le programme des Détenus Dangere (région de Québec)," internal document of the Canadian Penitentiary Service, p. 4.

(101) Ibid., p. 4.

(102) Ibid.

(103) *MPESC*, 11:43-44.

(104) *Montréal-Matin*, 28 February 1976.

(105) *MPESC*, 40:86-87.

(106) *MPESC*, 40:87.

(107) *MPESC*, 36:17.

(108) *MPESC*, 40:129.

(109) *L'Express*, no. 1280, p. 19, 25 January 1976.

(110) *Man Against Man: Brainwashing*, by Edgar H. Schein, M.I.T.

(111) *Criminals Can Be Brainwashed Now*, by James V. McConnell.

(112) *MPESC*, 14:27.

(113) "Programme d'apprentissage social," Carrefour Nouveau Monde, June 1975.

(114) *MPESC*, 36:18.

(115) *MPESC*, 36:11.

(116) *MPESC*, 36:20.

(117) *Report of the Sub-Committee on the Penitentiary System in Canada*, May 1977, paragraph 50, p. 12.

(118) *MPESC*, 40:76.

CRIMES OF THE SECRET POLICE

by **Robert Dion**

After four years and an expenditure of $10 million, the MacDonald Commission Report on the Royal Canadian Mounted Police was released. It includes a list of crimes committed by the secret police of Canada, implicating some 200 police agents. *The Report would have been "softer" without the Keable Commission Report in Quebec.* The Federal Government's Commission was forced to investigate matters that were not on its agenda. Why? What happened?

In a powerfully written book, Québec journalist and researcher Robert Dion deals with the role of the RCMP in Québec, the infiltration of trade unions, political groups, and the Parti Québecois plus various other crimes (what the media calls "wrong doings"). Dion covers the Keable Commission and its conflict with the MacDonald Commission. In a telling analysis, material is discussed which has not been dealt with in other books on the RCMP. Dion also analyzes the MacDonald Report with useful insights that can add to the vigilance needed when viewing the proposed new "national security agency." This analysis and information is imperative if we are to have a useful public debate and action.

Paperback ISBN: 0-919-619-56-2   **$ 9.95**
Hardcover ISBN: 0-919-619-57-0   **$19.95**
Contains: Canadian Shared Cataloguing in Publication Data
CRIMINOLOGY / SOC / CAN STUDIES

THE CITY AND RADICAL SOCIAL CHANGE

edited by
Dimitrios
Roussopoulos

What is the role of the city in determining the evolution of society as a whole? What perspective do people who fight to improve public transportation, housing, public health and related issues have? What are the results of the community-organising movement in cities like Mon-tréal? How have the concepts of participatory demo-cracy, decentralisation, and the creation of neigh-bourhood councils evolved?

With a focus on Montréal, the book examines through a collection of essays the dynamics of the community-organising movement and its impact on urban politics.

320 pages
Paperback ISBN: 0-919618-82-0   **$12.95**
Hardcover ISBN: 0-919618-83-9   **$20.95**
Contains: Canadian Shared Cataloguing in Publication Data
BLACK ROSE BOOKS No. H44

WOMEN & REVOLUTION

edited by Lydia Sargent

Women and Revolution deals with contemporary political theory and practice. It is a debate concerning the importance of patriarchy and sexism in industrialized societies — are sexual differences and kin relations as critical to social outcome as economic relations? What is the dynamic between class and sex? Is one or the other dominant? How do they interact? What are the implications for efforts at social change?

The principle essay to which all others respond — either criticizing it, extending, or attempting to improve it — is "The Unhappy Marriage of Marxism and Feminism" by Heidi Hartmann. Hartmann argues that class and patriarchy are equally important and that neither a narrow feminism nor an economistic Marxism will suffice to help us understand or change modern society — instead we need a theory that can integrate the two analyses.

Table of Contents include: Beyond the Unhappy Marriage: a critique of the Dual Systems Theory by Iris Young; Socialism, Feminism, and Gay / Lesbian Liberation by Christine Riddiough; The Incompatible Meange a Trois by Gloria Joseph; The Unhappy Marriage, can it be saved? by Carol Erlich; The First Division of Labour by Sandra Harding; Capitalism is an advanced stage of Patriarchy but Marxism is not Feminism by Azizah al-Hibri; Trial Separation or Something else? by Lise Vogel; Cultural Marxism: Nonsynchrony and feminist practice by Emily Hicks; From Private to Public Patriarchy by Carol Brown; The Marriage of Capitalist and Patriarchal Ideologies by Katie Stewart; Reform and / or Revolution — Towards a Unified Women's Movement by Zillah Eisenstein.

Paperback ISBN: 0-919619-19-8   **$ 9.95**
Hardcover ISBN: 0-919619-20-1   **$19.95**
Contains: Canadian Shared Cataloguing in Publication Data

THE FRENCH LEFT

A History and Overview
by Arthur Hirsh

Consisting of a new evaluation of the intellectual history of the contemporary Left in France, this book is an important contribution to understanding the debates that have had an international influence.

The works of Henri Leferve, Cornelius Castoriadis, Andre Gorz, Jean-Paul Sartre, Louis Althusser, Simone de Beauvoir, Nicos Poulantzas and other outstanding theorists are presented in separate chapters. Each thinker is presented by examining the particular contributions they made to the development of socialist theory and practice. This overview and history is brought together by the author in an analysis of eurocommunism and the crisis of Marxism on the one hand and the new social movements of the 1970s on the other. It includes an extensive bibliography.

Paperback ISBN: 0-919619-23-6 $ 9.95
Hardcover ISBN: 0-919619-24-4 $19.95

Printed by
the workers of
Editions Marquis, Montmagny, Que.
for
Black Rose Books Ltd.